Christianity:
The White Man's Religion?

The Great Lie: A Perversion of Biblical Truth!

Reclaiming Biblical Truth

TONY L. SCOTT

"I am black but comely, O ye daughters of Jerusalem, as the tents of Kedar, as the curtains of Solomon. Look not upon me, because I am black because the sun hath looked upon me..."
(Song of Solomon 1:5,6 KJV)

ISBN (Paperback) - 979-8-9929197-0-7
ISBN (Hard Cover) - 979-8-9885933-9-3

For more information or permissions, please contact the author:
redeemedwriter718@gmail.com
tlmdscott2@gmail.com

Editor: This book was self-edited by the author.

Book Project Management:
Raindrop Creative, Inc. | StartWrite Publish Team
http://www.raindropbrand.com

Table of Contents

	Preface	1
	Introduction	3
Chapter 1	The Myth of Race and the Perversion of Biblical Truth	7
Chapter 2	Unmasking the Lie: The Curse of Canaan and the Evil of Racial Supremacy	25
Chapter 3	From Africa to Christ – One Blood One Image	39
Chapter 4	The War on Identity: Psychological and Spiritual Warfare	57
Chapter 5	How Did We Get Here? The African, Indigenous Americans, and European Journey Through Colonization	85
Chapter 6	Africa's Divine Connection: God's Word and Africa's Legacy	105
Chapter 7	Black Hebrew Israelites and Islam: Faith, Identity, and the Christian Response	137
Chapter 8	Restoring the Image: The Need for Redemption and Justice for All	153

Preface

In America (2025), there is a deep and growing racial division that cannot be ignored. The wounds of the past, compounded by centuries of injustice, inequality, and the belief in racial hierarchy, continue to affect how we relate to one another. The struggle for racial reconciliation remains one of the defining issues of our time. As a nation, we have not done a good job at all of fully understanding or confronting the history of racial oppression, particularly the legacy of slavery and its enduring impact on African Americans. For too long, the educational systems in America, in particular, have failed to adequately teach the truth about this history, leaving generations to grapple with the consequences of an incomplete and distorted narrative. Sadly, many want this to remain as so.

This book is written with the hope of offering a corrective—a way to reclaim biblical truth in the face of the falsehoods that have shaped our understanding of race, identity, and the history of this nation. It is a call to recognize that we are all created as one in Christ, no matter our ethnicity or the artificial construct of race that has often divided us. In Christ, we are united. We share a common humanity, one that was made in the image of God, and this truth transcends every societal boundary that has been drawn throughout history.

The history of African Americans—those who were forcibly brought to this land, enslaved, and who helped build this nation—has been tragically overlooked and misrepresented. This is not just a part of the past; it continues to shape the present. We must acknowledge the immense contributions of African Americans, and at the same time, we must confront the deep injustices that have been perpetuated against people of color. This is essential not only for understanding the true history of America but also for healing the divisions that persist in our society.

My hope in writing this book is to leave a legacy for not only my grandchildren and family but for all those I may influence—a legacy rooted in the much-needed truth of God's Word. I want them to know who they are in Christ, not based on the fleeting categories of ethnicity or race that have been constructed within misguided human ideology, but as those created in the image of God, loved by Him, and redeemed by the blood of Jesus. This book is an invitation to look beyond the narratives of division and to embrace the unity that is found in Christ alone.

Through this work, ***although I am not a Historian***, I seek to guide future generations toward a better understanding of our past, shared humanity and the truth of who we are in God. As we reclaim biblical truth, may we move beyond the limitations of earthly identities and come together as one people united under the banner of Christ, who has reconciled us to Himself and to one another.

To my lovely wife, Lisa. Thank you for your unwavering support and faithfulness.

Introduction

Throughout modern history, the world has grappled with the complexities of race, identity, and the deep-seated injustices that have emerged as a result of the fall of mankind. For centuries, these issues have been distorted and manipulated to serve agendas of power, division, and oppression, especially in the context of colonization and the abuse of religious truths. The Christian faith, rooted in the love and grace of God, has not been exempt from such manipulation. Yet, at its core, Christianity offers a message of unity, reconciliation, and redemption, regardless of "race," ethnicity, or background.

This book explores the myth of race, the historical and modern-day injustices faced by people of color, and the profound ways in which these issues have intersected with the truths of Scripture. From the perversion of biblical truth used to justify racial supremacy to the exploration of the legacy of Africa in God's divine plan, each chapter delves into the deep and complex relationship between faith, identity, and justice.

In Chapter 1, we begin by addressing the myth of race, examining how this concept, unsupported by Biblical truth, has led to the division and dehumanization of entire people groups. This distortion has been perpetuated through the misuse of Scripture, fueling racial injustice across the globe.

In Chapter 2, we unmask the ***Great lie*** of racial supremacy, particularly through the misapplication of the so-called curse of Canaan. The dangerous legacy of this misinterpretation continues to shape modern attitudes toward race, requiring a biblical reckoning with these false teachings.

Chapter 3 turns our focus toward Africa, emphasizing how Africa is not only central to the story of Scripture but also to the unfolding of God's redemptive work. We explore the theological truth that all people, regardless of origin, are created in the image of God, united by our shared humanity and need for salvation.

In Chapter 4, we examine the war on identity that continues to affect people of African descent, both in Africa and in the diaspora. The psychological and spiritual warfare waged through colonization and slavery has left deep scars, but the Gospel offers healing and a return to our true identity as imagers of God.

Chapter 5 takes a historical look at the journey of Africans, Indigenous Americans, and Europeans through colonization, exploring how these historical events shaped racial dynamics and distorted biblical truths, ultimately leaving a legacy of division that we still and greatly struggle with today.

Chapter 6 seeks to reconnect Africa with its divine purpose, highlighting how Africa's legacy in God's kingdom is not one of subjugation but of deep and eternal significance. Africa's historical and spiritual contributions to God's Word are foundational to understanding the gospel's reach and power across the world.

Chapter 7 dives into the rise of the Black Hebrew Israelite (BHI) and Muslim movements in America, examining how these belief systems have emerged in response to the history of oppression and injustice. We will see how they seek identity and purpose and how the Christian faith provides the ultimate answer to the search for truth, identity, and redemption.

Finally, Chapter 8 concludes by restoring the image of God in humanity. We are all created in the image of God, but due to sin, we are in need of redemption. This chapter emphasizes the importance of justice and the Christian call to act with compassion and love for all people, acknowledging our shared humanity and working toward true justice, both now and in the eternal kingdom of God.

This book is an invitation to rediscover the Biblical truths that unite us and to challenge the misconceptions that have perpetuated division and injustice. As we journey through history, theology, and cultural dynamics, with some recapitulation for emphasis, we will see that, in Christ, we are all one – united in our need for redemption, our call for justice, and our shared hope for an eternal future with God.

CHAPTER I

The Myth of Race and the Perversion of Biblical Truth

Mankind: One People, One Blood

Science affirms what the Bible has declared for millennia: humanity is one. Genetically, all human beings share 99.9% of the same DNA, with minor variations accounting for physical differences such as skin color, hair texture, and facial features. These differences are superficial and do not define separate races in a biological sense. In reality, there is only one human race, descended from the same original ancestors. The apostle Paul affirmed this truth when he preached in Athens:

"And (*God*) hath made of one blood all nations of men for to dwell on all the face of the earth, and hath determined the times before appointed, and the bounds of their habitation." (Acts 17:26, KJV)

The concept of separate races is not found in the Word of God. Instead, Scripture consistently refers to different nations and peoples, all created by God and equally accountable to Him. The idea of racial superiority is a man-made construct, a distortion of both Biblical truth and scientific reality.

The Creation of Race: A European Construct of Oppression

The concept of race as we understand it today did not exist in the ancient world. People were categorized by their tribes, nations, or languages, but not by skin color as a determinant of worth or hierarchy. The artificial division of humanity into racial categories emerged primarily during the European colonial era as a means to justify conquest, enslavement, and economic exploitation.

European powers, under great spiritual deception, began to view themselves as inherently superior to other peoples, particularly Africans. This mindset gave rise to the ***Doctrine of Discovery***, a belief that European*, so-called* Christians, operating under the banner of Christendom, sanctioned by the Catholic Church, had the divine right to claim lands inhabited by non-Europeans and to subjugate them under the guise of spreading civilization and *so-called,* twisted or perverted Christianity. This doctrine became the foundation for European colonial expansion, the Transatlantic Slave Trade, and the brutal exploitation of Africans and Africa.

*[Please feel free to insert the wording **"so-called"** before Christians and Christianity, where I do not rightly do so throughout this study to distinguish between the true Christian faith and the perversion, abuse and misuse of it].*

"Woe unto them that call evil good, and good evil; that put darkness for light, and light for darkness; that put bitter for sweet, and sweet for bitter!" (Isaiah 5:20, KJV)

The Curse of Canaan: A Biblical Distortion Used to Justify Slavery

One of the most egregious perversions of Scripture used to justify the enslavement of Africans (Blacks) was the misapplication of the curse of Canaan. The biblical account in Genesis states that after Noah became drunk, his son Ham saw his father's nakedness. As a result, Noah pronounced a curse—not on Ham himself, but on Ham's son, Canaan:

"And he said, Cursed be Canaan; a servant of servants shall he be unto his brethren." (Genesis 9:25, KJV)

This curse was specific to Canaan, one of Ham's four sons, whose descendants later settled in the land that became Canaan (modern-day Israel and Palestine). Nowhere in Scripture is this curse extended to all of Ham's descendants, let alone to all Black or African people. Yet, European theologians and slave traders twisted this passage to claim that all Africans were divinely destined for servitude. This false doctrine became a cornerstone for justifying the African slave trade and the dehumanization of Black people.

The true Biblical record contradicts this distortion. Ham's other descendants—Cush (Nubia, modern Sudan), Mizraim (Egypt), and Put (Libya)—were never cursed. In fact, Africa plays a significant role in biblical history, often being a place of refuge and prominence.

Moses married a Cushite woman (Numbers 12:1), and the Jewish prophet Zephaniah was of Cushite descent (Zephaniah 1:1). Furthermore, when Jesus was a child, His family fled to Egypt for safety (Matthew 2:13-15), demonstrating that Africa was not a land of cursed people but a land of divine purpose and a people of color.

"Are ye not as children of the Cushites unto me, O children of Israel? saith the Lord" (Amos 9:7). Reading this text in context suggests God is Sovereign over all nations, and His care is for all people. However, some presuppose that this text speaks to the skin color of the Israelites. Exodus 12:38 regarding God's deliverance of Israel reads – **"A mixed multitude also went up with them…"** It is not beyond reason that before and after God's deliverance, there were marriages (ethnic blending) among these people with varying skin pigmentation or melanin. Furthermore, this **"mixed multitude"** is indicative of God's grace extended to *whoever* would follow after Him.

Europe's Spiritual Deception and the Quest for Domination

Fueled by the lie of racial superiority, European nations embarked on centuries of conquest, colonization, and enslavement. Under the guise of spreading Christianity, they stripped entire civilizations of their autonomy, culture, and dignity. This was not the work of Christ but of men operating under the influence of greed, pride, and spiritual deception.

Jesus Himself denounced such behavior:

"But Jesus called them unto him, and said, Ye know that the princes of the Gentiles exercise dominion over them, and they that are great exercise authority upon them. But it shall not be so among you: but whosoever will be great among you, let him be your minister; And whosoever will be chief among you, let him be your servant." (Matthew 20:25-27, KJV)

The enslavement and brutalization of African people were *not in alignment* with the teachings of Christ, who commanded His followers to *love their neighbors as themselves* (Mark 12:31). Instead, the colonizers and European Catholic Church aligned itself with empire and oppression, distorting the gospel for political and economic gain.

The Perverted Use of Scripture to Justify Slavery

During the Transatlantic Slave Trade and the period of chattel slavery in the Americas and beyond, European enslavers manipulated Scripture to justify their brutal system of oppression.

One of the most frequently cited verses was:

"Slaves, obey your earthly masters with respect and fear, and with sincerity of heart, just as you would obey Christ." (Ephesians 6:5, NIV)

This passage, along with similar verses, was *ripped from its original context and weaponized* to enforce submission among enslaved Africans.

"Slaves, obey your masters in everything; and do it, not only when their eye is on you and to curry their favor, but with sincerity of heart and reverence for the Lord." (Colossians 3:22, NIV)

"Teach slaves to be subject to their masters in everything, to try to please them, not to talk back to them." (Titus 2:9, NIV)

"Slaves, in reverent fear of God submit yourselves to your masters, not only to those who are good and considerate, but also to those who are harsh." (1 Peter 2:18, NIV)

However, in its proper Biblical and historical context, these scriptures *did not* endorse race-based, perpetual chattel slavery, where people were viewed as property and not human beings.

In the Greco-Roman world, servitude was often a temporary condition and was not based on race. Many people sold themselves into servitude to pay debts, and they could eventually earn their freedom. Additionally, biblical servanthood included protections for the servant's well-being. The Torah commanded fair treatment of servants, including their release after six years:

"If you buy a Hebrew servant, he is to serve you for six years. But in the seventh year, he shall go free, without paying anything." (Exodus 21:2, NIV)

"If any of your people—Hebrew men or women—sell themselves to you and serve you six years, in the seventh year you must let them go free. And when you release them, do not send them away empty-handed. Supply them liberally from your flock, your threshing floor and your winepress. Give to them as the Lord your God has blessed you. Remember that you were slaves in Egypt and the Lord your God redeemed you. That is why I give you this command today." (Deuteronomy 15:12-15, NIV)

Furthermore, Paul's letter to Philemon regarding the runaway slave Onesimus challenged the idea of slavery as a permanent institution. Paul instructed Philemon to welcome Onesimus:

"No longer as a slave, but better than a slave, as a dear brother. He is very dear to me but even dearer to you, both as a fellow man and as a brother in the Lord." (Philemon 1:16, NIV)

These principles were ignored by European enslavers who claimed to be Christians yet perpetuated one of history's greatest evils. Considering the Bible's misuse, the enslaved Africans who knew better and ***who embraced the truth of Scripture,*** in many cases, were not accepted as fully Christian or acknowledged at all by their enslavers and were even denied baptism. This, however, was **not the beginning of Christianity among African people.** While many enslaved Africans were forcibly introduced to Christianity by their captors, history reveals that **some had already embraced the Christian faith long before their enslavement.** This created somewhat of a dilemma for some enslavers. To address the problem most of them totally disregarded this truth as well. Although a few enslaved Africans were freed according to certain laws that protected Christians, these laws or practices were soon amended or overridden. I must also acknowledge that along with Christianity, there were other beliefs that Africans also held on to.

It was kingdoms such as Kongo and Ndongo in Central Africa had welcomed Christianity through missionary efforts prior to the transatlantic slave trade. **In East Africa, Ethiopian and Nubian Christians had worshiped Christ for centuries,** maintaining a faith tradition independent of European influence. **This reality challenges the false narrative that Christianity was exclusively imposed upon Africans by Europeans.** Some of those who were chained and brought to America carried with them a faith in the same Christ their oppressors falsely claimed to serve. They knew the difference between the Gospel of liberation and the distorted Christianity of their enslavers. The enslaved who already knew Christ did not receive Him from the hands of those who shackled them; instead, they clung to the truth they had before bondage and recognized the hypocrisy of their oppressors.

"Woe to those who make unjust laws, to those who issue oppressive decrees, to deprive the poor of their rights and withhold justice from the oppressed of my people, making widows their prey and robbing the fatherless." (Isaiah 10:1-2, NIV)

The Slave Bible: A Tool of Oppression

To further control enslaved Africans, European enslavers and clergy created a heavily edited version of the Bible known as the "Slave Bible." This version, published in 1807 by the Society for the Conversion of Negro Slaves, removed vast portions of Scripture that spoke of liberation, justice, and God's opposition to oppression.

The Slave Bible omitted nearly 90% of the Old Testament and 50% of the New Testament. Scriptures such as:

"Anyone who kidnaps someone is to be put to death, whether the victim has been sold or is still in the kidnapper's possession." (Exodus 21:16, NIV)

Were completely removed:

The story of Moses leading the Israelites out of Egypt (Exodus 3-14) was also erased, as it symbolized freedom from bondage.

However, passages that seemed to enforce servitude, such as **Ephesians 6:5 and Colossians 3:22**, were left intact. This manipulation of Scripture served to pacify enslaved people, discouraging resistance and rebellion while keeping many spiritually and psychologically subjugated.

This gross distortion of God's Word stands as a testimony to the spiritual deception of European colonizers and slaveholders. They feared the full gospel message because it proclaimed a *God who liberates the oppressed.* Yet, despite their oppressor's efforts, many enslaved Africans clung to the true message of Scripture—one of deliverance, justice, and God's unwavering presence in the suffering.

Jesus declared, "The Spirit of the Lord is upon me, because he has anointed me to proclaim good news to the poor. He has sent me to proclaim freedom for the prisoners and recovery of sight for the blind, to set the oppressed free." (Luke 4:18, NIV)

Jesus offered spiritual liberation from the forces of darkness immediately. However, remember that chattel slavery was not the practice of His time. That said, deliverance from oppression of all sorts is what Jesus preached. However, it would be through changed hearts, as a result of the indwelling Holy Spirit, that much-needed change would ultimately come, however, not without resistance. But what we must remember is that we live in a world influenced by wicked principalities and amongst people who remain sinful in heart, with each of us in varying measures prone to sin or who will engage in sinful acts.

The Complexity of Black Identity in the Bible and History

The European-imposed definition of Blackness has somewhat varied throughout history, yet it has consistently been used to justify subjugation. In the United States, the one-drop rule dictated that any person with even a trace of African ancestry was considered Black. This rule reinforced white supremacy by ensuring that mixed-race individuals, regardless of how they looked, were denied the privileges of whiteness.

However, this same concept of Black identity can be applied to Biblical figures who, by geographical origin and ancestry, would be considered Black by this definition of the one-drop rule. Clearly, many individuals in the Bible were of African descent or had significant African lineage.

Distinctively Black Figures in the Bible

Some biblical figures are described with characteristics that align with what enslavers, colonizers, or Europeans have defined as Black features. These include dark skin and tightly coiled hair, though variations of Blackness exist.

- Cushites (Nubians/Sudanese): The Cushites were descendants of Cush, the son of Ham.

"The sons of Ham: Cush, Egypt, Put, and Canaan." (Genesis 10:6, NIV)

The region of Cush, located in modern-day Sudan, was known for its dark-skinned inhabitants.

The prophet Zephaniah was of Cushite descent:

"The word of the Lord that came to Zephaniah son of Cushi, the son of Gedaliah, the son of Amariah, the son of Hezekiah during the reign of Josiah son of Amon king of Judah." (Zephaniah 1:1, NIV)

Moses' wife was described as a Cushite:

"Miriam and Aaron began to talk against Moses because of his Cushite wife, for he had married a Cushite." (Numbers 12:1, NIV)

Interracial Unions and the Mixed Lineage of Biblical Figures

By the same standard used by European enslavers, many biblical figures could be considered Black due to interracial unions throughout history.

- Joseph's Children (Ephraim and Manasseh, Black by European definition):

"Pharaoh gave Joseph the name Zaphenath-Paneah and gave him Asenath daughter of Potiphera, priest of On, to be his wife. And Joseph went throughout the land of Egypt." (Genesis 41:45, NIV) These two sons made up the twelve tribes of Israel. (Genesis 48:4,5 and 48:13-20)

- Solomon's Lineage:

"And when the queen of Sheba heard of the fame of Solomon concerning the name of the Lord, she came to prove him with hard questions." (1 Kings 10:1, KJV)

Thus, when applying the one-drop rule imposed by Europeans, a significant number of biblical figures could be classified as Black. This challenges the whitewashed depictions of biblical characters seen in Western art and reinforces the fact that Africa and its descendants have always been central to the biblical narrative.

"Can the Ethiopian/Cushites change his skin or the leopard its spots? Neither can you do good who are accustomed to doing evil." (Jeremiah 13:23, NIV)

This rhetorical question recognizes the distinctiveness of Cushites (Nubians/Sudanese) in the Biblical world. It affirms that Blackness was acknowledged in Scripture, not as a curse, but as an inherent part of human diversity.

The Shulamite woman in the Song of Solomon embraces her beauty:

"I am black but comely, O ye daughters of Jerusalem, as the tents of Kedar, as the curtains of Solomon. Look not upon me, because I am black, because the sun hath looked upon me…" (S.O.S. 1:5,6 KJV)

The Diversity of Blackness in the Ancient World

Because of tribal intermarriages (ethnic blending) and migrations, Blackness has always encompassed a broad range of physical features. Some individuals were ***distinctively*** Black with dark skin and tightly coiled hair, while others—due to centuries of genetic blending—bore features that might resemble Europeans. Despite this variation, these people are to be understood as non-European and thus part of the global community of people of color.

The biblical world, particularly in the Old and New Testaments, was primarily composed of Black and brown people – people of various hues. The regions of ancient Israel, Canaan, Egypt, Nubia (modern-day Sudan), and surrounding territories were home to various African and Semitic peoples whose physical appearances would have aligned with what we recognize today as Black or non-European.

Greek and Roman Influence in the Middle East and North Africa

The significant European influence in the Middle East and North Africa (the Afro-Asiatic region) did not occur until the expansion of the Greek and Roman empires. Alexander the Great's conquests (4th century BC) brought Hellenistic (Greek) cultural and genetic influence into the region, but this influence, though profound, remained limited in terms of numbers or European population. The same was true of the Roman Empire, which expanded into North Africa and the Levant.

However, despite their presence, Greeks and Romans (Europeans) were never the dominant ethnic groups in these regions, even though there were also prior Mediterranean-European interactions throughout the Levant. The vast majority of people remained ethnically and culturally tied to their indigenous African and Semitic roots. Even during the height of Greco-Roman rule, the Middle East and North Africa were still populated primarily by Black and brown people, reinforcing the truth that the Biblical world was not a European-dominated region but a reflection of the diverse, richly melanated populations of the time. Again, reasoning would dictate that there were mixed marriages of Europeans with the indigenous people of these regions – hence producing more Blacks or people of color.

The Foundations of White Supremacy and Scientific Racism

The ideology of white supremacy was not just a social construct but a deliberate pseudoscientific attempt to justify European domination. Two individuals, Johann Friedrich Blumenbach and Joseph Arthur de Gobineau, played critical roles in formulating racial classifications that provided the so-called intellectual foundation for racism.

Johann Friedrich Blumenbach: The Father of Racial Classification

Johann Friedrich Blumenbach (1752–1840), a German physician and naturalist, is often credited as the "father of racial classification." His work,

On the Natural Varieties of Mankind (1775), divided humanity into five racial categories:

1. **Caucasian (Europeans, particularly those from the Caucasus region)**
2. **Mongolian (Asians)**
3. **Malayan (Pacific Islanders and Southeast Asians)**
4. **Ethiopian (Africans)**
5. **American (Indigenous peoples of the Americas)**

Blumenbach regarded the "Caucasian" race as the original and most beautiful of all races, implying a natural superiority. He derived the term from the people of the Caucasus Mountains (modern-day Georgia and Russia), whom he deemed physically ideal. This classification reinforced *the false belief – the Great Lie* that Europeans were the standard of human perfection, while non-European races were considered inferior deviations.

Although Blumenbach himself did not promote slavery or racial oppression, his classification system was later weaponized by white supremacists to justify colonialism, enslavement, and segregation.

Joseph Arthur de Gobineau and the Scientific Race Theory

Joseph Arthur de Gobineau (1816–1882), a French aristocrat and writer, took Blumenbach's racial ideas further by promoting scientific racism— *the false notion* that race determines intelligence, moral capacity, and social worth. In his work An Essay on the Inequality of the Human Races (1853–1855), Gobineau argued that civilization's success depended on the purity of the White (Aryan) race. He asserted that racial mixing led to the decline of societies, fueling fears of miscegenation (ethnic blending) among European elites.

Gobineau's writings became foundational to white supremacist movements, influencing Nazi ideology and 20th-century eugenics programs that sought to control reproduction among non-white populations. His work justified European imperialism, apartheid, and segregationist policies, further entrenching the belief in racial hierarchies.

The Legacy of Scientific Racism

Blumenbach and Gobineau were not alone in shaping racial ideology. Other figures, such as:

- Carl Linnaeus (1707–1778) – Developed a racial classification in his taxonomy (racial classification) of human beings, linking race to personality traits.

- Herbert Spencer (1820–1903) – Coined the phrase "survival of the fittest" and applied Darwinian evolution to justify social and racial inequalities.

- Francis Galton (1822–1911) – Founder of the eugenics movement, which sought to "improve" the human race by controlling the reproduction of those deemed inferior.

These sordid and devious theories provided the corrupt intellectual basis for racism, colonial oppression, and the atrocities committed under white supremacist regimes. From the Transatlantic Slave Trade to Jim Crow laws in America, these ideas permeated legal, social, and religious institutions, distorting Biblical truth to maintain sinful systems of white dominance.

Closing Remarks on Chapter 1

As we conclude this chapter, it is clear that race—as defined by European colonialists—was never a Biblical or scientific truth but a social construct designed to justify oppression. The Scriptures never promote racial superiority but instead affirm the unity of all humanity.

"From one man He made all the nations, that they should inhabit the whole earth; and he marked out their appointed times in history and the boundaries of their lands." (Acts 17:26, NIV)

The great deception of white supremacy was not just a cultural phenomenon but a direct attack on God's creation. European colonizers took Biblical texts out of context to validate their racial hierarchy, using misinterpretations of Scripture, an evil and sinful wrong to suppress and oppress Black and Indigenous peoples. Yet, the Bible itself refutes these ideas, affirming that all people—regardless of their skin color—are created in God's image.

"So God created mankind in his own image, in the image of God he created them; male and female he created them." (Genesis 1:27, NIV)

The racial division we see today is not a divine order but a historical perversion of Biblical truth. Christianity was never meant to be a "white man's religion." Rather, from its roots in the ancient Middle East and Africa, the faith has always been a global movement centered on God's love for all people.

This first chapter has laid the groundwork for understanding how racial deception was woven into Western Society and Christianity. As we continue through this book, we will further expose the lies that have been used to distort the faith and reclaim the Biblical truth that Christianity is not, nor has it ever been, the exclusive religion of white Europeans or anyone for that matter.

CHAPTER 2

Unmasking the Lie: The Curse of Canaan and the Evil of Racial Supremacy

The First Humans and Their Skin Tone

Genesis 2:7 states:

"And the Lord God formed man of the dust of the ground, and breathed into his nostrils the breath of life, and man became a living soul." (KJV)

This verse provides a crucial foundation for understanding the physical composition of the first human, Adam. The phrase "dust of the ground" is significant because the soil in many regions of the ancient Near East and Africa ranges in color from deep reddish-brown to dark brown or black. Given that Adam was formed from this soil, it is reasonable to conclude that he possessed melanin, the natural pigment responsible for darker skin tones.

Melanin plays a vital role in protecting the skin from ultraviolet radiation and is predominantly found in people of African, Middle Eastern, and Indigenous descent. Since Adam and Eve were the first humans, created to populate the earth, their skin would have been richly pigmented, adapted for the sun-drenched environment of early civilization.

The Linguistic Connection: Adam, Adom, and Adamah

The name Adam (or description) in Hebrew carries deep linguistic and symbolic significance. It is closely related to adamah, which means "ground" or "earth," directly tying the first man to the soil from which he was formed. This connection reinforces the idea that Adam's complexion reflected the darker, reddish-brown hues of the fertile earth.

Additionally, the Hebrew word adom, meaning "red" or "ruddy," further emphasizes this association. This term does not necessarily refer to a pale or light-skinned complexion, as some have mistakenly assumed, but rather to a rich, earthy tone—akin to the deep red and brown hues of natural clay and soil. Many African and Middle Eastern cultures have historically described various shades of brown skin as "red," further supporting this interpretation.

Esau and His Distinctive Appearance

Genesis 25:25 states:

"And the first came out red, all over like a hairy garment; and they called his name Esau." (KJV)

Esau's unique description sets him apart from his brother, making it clear that his complexion was distinct. The Hebrew word used for "red" here is admoni, which is derived from adom, meaning red or ruddy. If Esau's relatives and, more specifically, his brother Jacob had the same skin tone as him, his redness would not have been noteworthy. Instead, this distinction implies that biblical peoples, including Adam and his descendants, were likely brown or dark-skinned, making Esau's unique red tone stand out. Just the same, his family and those of the region were all people of color.

Esau's description serves as a contrast to Adam's name. While both terms are related to the earth, Adam's association with adamah suggests a rich, dark-hued complexion, whereas Esau's admoni designation indicates an unusually reddish tone. This contrast further challenges the Eurocentric portrayals of Biblical figures as white and underscores the reality that the first humans were people of color.

The Genetic Connection: Human Origins and the Spread of Nations

Modern genetics and DNA studies have overwhelmingly traced human origins back to Africa. Scientists studying mitochondrial DNA—the genetic material passed down from mother to child—have identified what they call "Mitochondrial Eve," a common maternal ancestor from whom all humans today descend. This genetic marker points to Africa as the birthplace of humanity, aligning with the Biblical account of Adam and Eve.

The study of Y-chromosomal DNA, passed from father to son, also supports an African origin. These findings reinforce the Biblical assertion that mankind originated from a singular creation event, with Adam as the first man, formed from the dust of the earth (Genesis 2:7):

"Then the Lord God formed man of the dust of the ground, and breathed into his nostrils the breath of life, and man became a living soul."

The soil of this region is rich in dark, reddish-brown hues, lending further support to the idea that Adam, the first man, had a complexion reflecting the earth from which he was formed.

The Sons of Noah and the Re-Population of the Earth

After the flood, humanity was re-established through Noah's three sons—Shem, Ham, and Japheth—who became the ancestors of the major people groups that spread across the earth (Genesis 9:18-19):

"The sons of Noah who went forth from the ark were Shem, Ham, and Japheth. Ham was the father of Canaan. These three were the sons of Noah, and from them the whole earth was populated."

Each son's descendants settled in distinct regions (actual borders are not known and very likely didn't exist), shaping the early civilizations of the post-flood world:

1. Ham – The father of Cush (Nubia/Sudan), Mizraim (Egypt), Put (Libya), and Canaan. His descendants primarily settled in Africa and parts of the Middle East, particularly along the Nile and in the land of Canaan. Cush, often translated as Ethiopia (in Greek, meaning a Black person), is better identified with Nubia, modern Sudan. The Hamitic nations played a significant role in early-world civilization, including Egypt, which was one of the most advanced cultures of antiquity.

2. Shem – The father of the Semitic peoples, including the Hebrews, Arabs, and Assyrians. His lineage includes Eber, from whom the name "Hebrew" is derived, and ultimately leads to Abraham, Isaac,

Jacob, and the Israelite nation. The Semitic people occupied the Middle East, particularly Mesopotamia, Arabia, and later, the land of Israel. These were people of color.

3. Japheth – The father of the Indo-European peoples. His descendants spread into Europe, Anatolia (modern Turkey), and parts of Central Asia. These peoples later formed the Greco-Roman civilizations and the northern Eurasian groups. It is speculated that, over time, their skinned tone (whiteness) was caused by the cooler climate and other environmental factors. Additionally, these physical distinctions are also believed to be the result of limited gene flow among these varied and isolated people groups.

God's Plan for Humanity's Dispersion

The dispersion of Noah's descendants was not accidental but part of God's divine plan. In Genesis 11, after the Tower of Babel incident, God confused human language, forcing people to spread out across the earth according to their familial groupings. This dispersion led to the formation of various nations, fulfilling God's command for humanity to **"be fruitful, multiply, and fill the earth" (Genesis 9:1).**

This division, however, was not meant to create racial hierarchies. The concept of race, as a classification system rooted in skin color and physical features, is, in fact, a human construct, not a Biblical one. In God's design, ethnic diversity was a reflection of His creativity and sovereignty, not a justification for division, oppression, or superiority.

The Misrepresentation of Ham's Lineage: Erasing the Lie of a Cursed People

A long-standing falsehood has permeated history—the claim that Ham's descendants were cursed and that this supposed curse justified the enslavement of African people. This distortion of Scripture has been used to defend racial hierarchies, colonial oppression, and the Transatlantic Slave Trade. However, when we closely examine the Biblical text, we find that the curse was not upon Ham himself or all his descendants but specifically upon Canaan, one of Ham's four sons.

Genesis 9:25 records Noah's words:

"Cursed be Canaan; a servant of servants shall he be to his brothers."

This curse had nothing to do with the entire lineage of Ham, nor did it prophesy the subjugation of African people. Ham had four sons—Cush, Mizraim, Put, and Canaan (Genesis 10:6)—and it was only Canaan, the ancestor of the Canaanite people, who was mentioned in Noah's pronouncement.

Who Were the Canaanites?

The Canaanites were a people who inhabited the land of Canaan – hence the Canaanite people, a region corresponding to modern-day Israel, Palestine, Lebanon, Jordan, and parts of Syria. The Bible describes the Canaanites as a mixture of various tribes, including the Hittites, Jebusites, Amorites, Girgashites, Hivites, and Perizzites (Exodus 3:8). These people were known for their pagan religious practices, which often included idolatry, temple prostitution, and child sacrifices to gods like Baal and Molech.

God warned Israel about the wickedness of these nations and commanded them to drive them out (Deuteronomy 7:1-2). This was not about racial superiority but about preserving the spiritual purity of God's chosen people – the Israelites or Jewish people.

The Fulfillment of the Curse Upon Canaan

The prophetic fulfillment of Noah's curse upon Canaan came through Israel's conquest of the Promised Land. God had promised Abraham that his descendants would inherit the land of Canaan (Genesis 15:18-21), and centuries later, under Joshua's leadership, Israel took possession of the land.

Joshua 9:23 recounts how some Canaanites, specifically the Gibeonites, were subjected to forced labor:

"Now therefore, you are cursed, and some of you shall never cease to be slaves, cutters of wood and drawers of water for the house of my God."

This servitude fulfilled the prophetic words spoken by Noah, but it had nothing to do with Africans or the Transatlantic Slave Trade. The descendants of Canaan were Middle Eastern peoples who inhabited the land that God promised to Abraham's lineage.

Additionally, even though many Canaanites were conquered, not all were exterminated. Some assimilated into Israelite society, and others continued to exist alongside the Israelites. The curse was a specific historical judgment upon the Canaanites due to their sinful practices and opposition to God's people, not an eternal condemnation of any racial or ethnic group.

The Perpetuation of the Lie and the Spiritual Wickedness Behind It

The Transatlantic Slave Trade and the systems of oppression that followed were built upon the foundation of the **Great Lie**—the belief in racial superiority. The European colonizers, slave traders, and racist theologians who justified slavery twisted Scripture and perpetuated falsehoods to maintain power and economic gain. But why has this lie—this hellish and satanic deception—continued to persist even in modern times?

The Persistence of a Satanic Deception

Despite the abolition of chattel slavery, the racial hierarchy established during that era did not simply disappear. The ideology that fueled slavery—white supremacy, racial classification, and social stratification—was institutionalized into laws, education, religious teachings, and economic systems. Therefore, there remains a prideful spiritual stronghold on the minds of many.

This deception continued through:

1. **Theological Justifications** – Many churches refused to repent of their complicity in slavery. They instead reinforced segregationist doctrines, claiming that certain races were divinely ordained to serve others.

2. **Scientific Racism** – The false racial theories propagated by figures like Johann Blumenbach and Joseph Arthur de Gobineau (as previously discussed) were further developed into eugenics, leading to forced sterilizations and discriminatory policies.

3. **Systemic Oppression** – After slavery ended, new systems, such as Jim Crow laws, apartheid, redlining, and mass incarceration, were put in place to continue subjugation under different names.

4. **Cultural Reinforcement** – The media, literature, and educational institutions were manipulated to distort history and reinforce racial superiority. For example, history books often depicted Africa as a land of savages in need of European civilization, rather than recognizing its rich cultures, kingdoms, and contributions to the world.

The persistence of this **Great lie** is not merely human ignorance or malice—it is a spiritual deception and stronghold on the minds of many Europeans orchestrated by pride and even Satan himself. The devil is described as the father of lies (John 8:44), and he has used racial division as one of his most effective tools to corrupt humanity, pit people against each other, and hinder the truth of God's Word of unity and oneness.

Exodus 21:16: A Divine Condemnation of Slavery

One of the most damning rebukes of slavery comes from Exodus 21:16, which states:

"Whoever steals a man and sells him, and anyone found in possession of him, shall be put to death."

This scripture clearly condemns the act of kidnapping people and selling them into slavery. The Transatlantic Slave Trade was rooted in the very crime that God Himself declared punishable by death. Slave traders and colonizers who claimed to be Christian were in direct violation of God's law, proving that their actions were not inspired by biblical truth, but rather by demonic deception and greed.

The Spiritual Wickedness Behind Racial Oppression

Ephesians 6:12 reminds us that the struggle for justice and truth is not just a physical battle but a spiritual one:

"For we do not wrestle against flesh and blood, but against the rulers, against the authorities, against the cosmic powers over this present darkness, against the spiritual forces of evil in the heavenly places."

The slave trade, colonization, racism, and oppression were not merely human failings—they were manifestations of a deeper spiritual battle overtaking the minds of all involved.

1. **Satan's Plan to Corrupt God's Image** – From the beginning, humans were created in the image of God (Genesis 1:26-27). By promoting racial division and slavery, Satan, through his human agents, sought to degrade and dehumanize people, leading them to believe that one group was inferior and another superior.

2. **The Perversion of Scripture** – Just as Satan twisted God's words in the Garden of Eden (Genesis 3:1), he has worked through false teachers and theologians to misinterpret Scripture in ways that justify oppression.

3. **The Disruption of God's Kingdom Vision** – God's plan has always been for all nations, tribes, and tongues to worship Him together (Revelation 7:9). The devil, knowing this, and through mankind's sinful disposition has sown division, hatred, and racism to hinder the gospel and distort the unity that God desires.

Breaking the Chains of Spiritual Deception

The truth of God's Word must be proclaimed in its fullness to counteract the lies that have persisted for generations. Recognizing that slavery and racism were tools of spiritual wickedness, we must reject any ideology that perpetuates racial superiority and embrace the Biblical truth that all humans are created equal in God's image.

The Biblical Vision of Unity

While history has been tainted by racial division and misinterpretations of Scripture, the Bible's ultimate message is one of *unity through Jesus.* The vision of God's kingdom is *inclusive, transcending race, nationality, and ethnic divisions.*

Revelation 7:9 paints a powerful picture of God's redemptive plan for all people:

"After this I looked, and behold, a great multitude that no one could number, from every nation, from all tribes and peoples and languages, standing before the throne and before the Lamb, clothed in white robes, with palm branches in their hands."

God's kingdom is multiethnic, embracing all who call upon His name. The idea that one race is superior to another is a human distortion and outright lie, not a biblical truth. The gospel of Jesus the Christ breaks down barriers, offering salvation to all nations, tribes, and tongues.

Closing Remarks of Chapter 2

As we conclude this chapter, it is crucial to reflect on the truths that have been unveiled and the deceptions that have been exposed. The history of humanity—beginning with Adam and Eve, extending through Noah's sons, and spanning the nations that descended from them—reveals God's sovereign plan for all people. Science confirms what Scripture already declared: that humanity originated from a common ancestry and that racial divisions were not ordained by God but rather constructed by lustful and prideful men seeking power.

The misuse of Noah's curse to justify the enslavement of African people was a satanic distortion of Biblical truth. Canaan—not Ham—was the one cursed, and his descendants' fate was fulfilled in Biblical prophecy, not in the Transatlantic Slave Trade. Despite this, white supremacists, slave traders, colonizers, and racist theologians manipulated Scripture to serve their own corrupt and ungodly agendas, perpetuating centuries of oppression built on a hellish lie.

God's Word, however, stands as the ultimate authority and truth. From Genesis to Revelation, the Bible presents a vision of unity, in which God calls people from every nation, tribe, and language to worship Him in harmony (Revelation 7:9). The spiritual wickedness and sinful failings of humanity that fueled slavery, racism, and oppression continues to manifest today, but as Believers, we are called to expose these works of darkness (Ephesians 5:11) and proclaim the truth of God's justice and love.

Let this chapter serve as a declaration of truth—that humanity was created as one people, in the image of God, and that no race is superior to another. Let it be a rebuke to the lies and deceptions that have justified oppression, and let it be a reminder that our ultimate allegiance is to the God of justice, truth, and unity – ***one in Him.***

May we be ambassadors of truth, rejecting falsehoods and embracing the Biblical vision of unity that God has ordained.

Consider the following Scripture:

1 What causes quarrels and what causes fights among you? Is it not this, that your passions are at war within you? 2 You desire and do not have, so you murder. You covet and cannot obtain, so you fight and quarrel. You do not have, because you do not ask. 3 You ask and do not receive, because you ask wrongly, to spend it on your passions.
(James 4:1-3)

CHAPTER 3

From Africa to Christ - One Blood One Image

The Genetic Connection: Scientific Evidence of Humanity's Origins

As we transition into Chapter 3, we shift our focus from not only our physical identity but, more importantly, our spiritual composition as beings created in the image of God. However, before diving into the depths of our spiritual identity, it is important ***to reinforce*** what scientific and genetic studies have revealed about humanity's physical origins, as these discoveries affirm what Scripture has long declared: ***that all humans share a common ancestry.***

For those unfamiliar with the scientific language of genetics, let us break down these studies in a way that is more accessible and practical for the layperson.

Mitochondrial Eve: The Mother of All Living

In the field of genetics, researchers have traced human ancestry through what is known as mitochondrial DNA (mtDNA), which is passed from mother to child with little variation over generations. This has led to the discovery of what scientists call Mitochondrial Eve, a single woman from whom all humans have descended through the maternal line.

Mitochondrial Eve indicates that all people today share a common female ancestor, and her genetic lineage has continued unbroken. Importantly, this research points to Africa as the geographical origin of humanity, confirming that the earliest human populations arose from this region.

Y-Chromosomal Adam: The Father of All Men

Similarly, Y-chromosomal DNA is inherited exclusively through the paternal line (from father to son). Genetic studies have also traced this lineage back to what is called Y-Chromosomal Adam, the most recent common ancestor of all men. Like Mitochondrial Eve, Y-Chromosomal Adam represents the single male lineage that has continued throughout human history. Again, research places the origins of this genetic line in Africa, reinforcing the same conclusions drawn from mtDNA studies.

Genetic Diversity and the Spread of Nations

One of the key findings in human genetics is that African populations have the greatest genetic diversity of any people on earth. This diversity suggests that humanity had its longest and earliest history in Africa before migrating outward to populate the rest of the world.

These findings align with Biblical history, particularly the dispersion of nations as described in Genesis 10 (the Table of Nations) and the events following the Tower of Babel (Genesis 11). According to Scripture, all nations ultimately descend from Noah's three sons, Shem, Ham, and Japheth, who repopulated the earth after the flood.

Scientific Evidence and Biblical Truth

What is striking is that modern genetic discoveries do not contradict Scripture but rather affirm it. The idea that all humans descend from one ancestral group is consistent with the Bible's declaration that all people come from Adam and Eve (Genesis 1:26-28).

Additionally, these findings dismantle racist ideologies that claim one group of people is inherently superior to another. Science confirms that race is a social construct rather than a biological reality, as all humans share 99.9% of the same DNA. The small variations in skin color, hair texture, and facial features are believed by some as the result of adaptations to different environments over time—not indicators of separate racial origins. Additionally, these physical distinctions are also believed to be the result of genetic isolation among the varied people groups.

Thus, whether viewed through the lens of science or Scripture, the truth remains the same: *humanity is one*. We are all descendants of the same ancestors, created by the same God, and called to recognize our unity rather than emphasize division.

Now, having established and restated the physical identity of mankind, we can turn our attention to the more profound question—our spiritual identity as children of God and what it truly means to be made in His image.

Imago Dei: The Divine Image in Humanity

The concept of being created in the image of God (Imago Dei) is one of the most profound theological truths in biblical revelation. It is first introduced in Genesis 1:26-27, where God declares:

"Then God said, 'Let Us make man in Our image, according to Our likeness; and let them have dominion over the fish of the sea, over the birds of the air, and over the cattle, over all the earth and over every creeping thing that creeps on the earth.' So God created man in His own image; in the image of God He created him; male and female He created them." (Genesis 1:26-27, NKJV)

This declaration distinguishes humanity from all other creation, revealing that man is not merely a biological entity but a spiritual being clothed in flesh designed to reflect God's nature. However, what does it truly mean to be created in God's image, and how does this extend beyond our physical form into our spiritual identity?

The Hebrew and Greek Understanding of "Image" and "Likeness"

To grasp the depth of the Imago Dei, or imagers of God, we must examine the original Hebrew and Greek words used in Scripture.

1. The Hebrew Word for "Image" – (Tselem)

- This word means "a resemblance, a shadow, or a representative figure."

- It implies that humanity was designed to reflect God's character and attributes, though not in a physical sense, since God is spirit (John 4:24).

- The word "tselem" is also used to describe idols in the Old Testament (e.g., Numbers 33:52), reinforcing the idea that humanity was meant to be God's living *representation* on earth—not as a carved image, but as a living being reflecting His glory.

2. The Hebrew Word for "Likeness" – (Demuth)

- This term means "similarity, model, pattern, or form."

- While "tselem" emphasizes *representation*, "Demuth" highlights the *relational* and functional aspects of God's image—our ability to think, *reason*, create, love, and exercise dominion.

- It suggests that humanity was not merely stamped with God's image but also empowered to function in accordance with His divine purpose.

3. The Greek Word for "Image" – (Eikón)

- In the New Testament, the Greek word "eikón" is used to describe Jesus as the exact representation of God:

"He is the image (eikón) of the invisible God, the firstborn over all creation." (Colossians 1:15)

- The use of "eikón" in reference to both Christ and humanity underscores that we were originally created to reflect the divine nature, and through Christ, that image is being restored (Romans 8:29).

What Does It Mean to Be Made in God's Image?

1. We Are Spiritual Beings with a Divine Purpose

Since God is spirit (John 4:24), our true identity is not merely physical but spiritual. Being made in His image means we were **designed for** *relationship with Him. We were not meant to function apart from God but to walk in communion with Him,* carrying out His will on earth.

- Ecclesiastes 3:11 says that God has placed eternity in our hearts, meaning that our souls long for something beyond the material world.

- Acts 17:28 states, **"In Him we live and move and have our being,"** affirming that our true existence and life are found in God alone.

2. We Possess Moral and Rational Capacities

Unlike animals, humans have a moral conscience, the ability to reason, and an innate understanding of justice and righteousness. This reflects God's holy nature and His desire for truth, love, and righteousness to govern creation.

- Romans 2:14-15 explains that even those who do not have the Law have the work of the Law written on their hearts, showing that God's moral nature is imprinted within us.

- Isaiah 1:18 declares, **"Come now, and let us reason together, says the Lord,"** showing that our ability to think, discern, and engage in moral reasoning comes from being made in God's image.

3. We Are Given Authority and Dominion

Genesis 1:26-28 reveals that part of being made in God's image involves dominion over the earth. This is not a license to exploit but rather a call to stewardship within His kingdom, a kingdom without physical borders.

- Psalm 8:5-6 says, **"You have made him a little lower than the angels and crowned him with glory and honor. You have made him to have dominion over the works of Your hands; You have put all things under his feet."**

- This means that humanity was entrusted with managing God's creation as His representatives. But it is ultimately fulfilled in Jesus and His rule.

4. We Were Created for Eternal Fellowship with God

Because we are made in God's image, we were designed for eternal communion with Him. However, sin corrupted this image (Genesis 3), separating humanity from God. But through Jesus Christ, the true image of God and His Father, this relationship is restored.

- 2 Corinthians 3:18 states that we are being transformed into the image of Christ, meaning that salvation restores what was lost in the Fall.

- Romans 8:29 says that those who are in Christ are predestined to be conformed to the image of the Son, showing that God's ultimate goal is to restore us fully to our intended state of holiness and righteousness.

The Ultimate Expression of the Imago Dei: Jesus Christ

While all humans bear God's image, Jesus Christ is the perfect and complete representation as the imager of His Father.

"The Son is the radiance of God's glory and the exact representation of His being." (Hebrews 1:3)

Jesus did not merely bear God's image—He is *the very image of God in human flesh.* Through Him, we see what it means to be truly human.

What does this mean for us?

- Through faith in Jesus Christ, we are renewed in knowledge according to the image of our Creator (Colossians 3:10).

- We are being transformed into His likeness from glory to glory (2 Corinthians 3:18).

- Our destiny is not only to reflect God's image but to be fully restored into the righteousness and holiness for which we were originally created (Ephesians 4:24).

Living in the Reality of the Imago Dei

To be created in God's image is not merely a theological concept—it is our spiritual reality. We are:

✓ **Spiritual beings designed for communion with God.**

✓ **Moral beings capable of righteousness and justice.**

✓ **Rational beings endowed with wisdom and creativity.**

✓ **Dominion-bearers called to steward God's creation.**

✓ **Eternal beings destined for union with God through Christ.**

Understanding the Imago Dei should transform the way we see ourselves, others, and our purpose in the world. Our true identity is not rooted in race, nationality, or social status—it is found in God alone, and through Christ, we are being restored to the full glory of His divine image.

The Unique and Eternally Existing Son of God: The Embodiment of Mankind

The Christian doctrine of the Incarnation teaches that Jesus Christ, the *Unique* and eternally existing Son of God, took on human flesh to redeem humanity. This act was a profound demonstration of God's love and His plan for salvation. The Apostle John writes in John 1:14, **"And the Word became flesh and dwelt among us, and we have seen His glory, glory as of the only Son from the Father, full of grace and truth."** This verse captures the essence of the Incarnation — God Himself, through His Son, became fully human while He (Jesus) yet remained fully divine.

Theologically, this means that Jesus was not merely a man who received divine power or was divinely inspired; He was the eternal Word (Logos), as described in the first chapter of John's Gospel, who, from all eternity, existed with God and as God. John 1:1-2 states, **"In the beginning was the Word, and the Word was with God, and the Word was God. He was in the beginning with God."** This underscores that Jesus' existence was not initiated at His birth in Bethlehem but spans eternity past. When

He **"put on flesh,"** He chose to enter into the world of humanity, living among us as a man, but still fully God.

The Incarnation and the Physical Nature of Jesus

When the Word (Jesus) became flesh, it is important to note that Jesus – the Unique or eternally existing Son of God assumed a real, physical human body. He took on the embodiment of mankind *in all its frailty*, except for sin. Hebrews 4:15 affirms, **"For we do not have a high priest who is unable to sympathize with our weaknesses, but one who in every respect has been tempted as we are, yet without sin."** Jesus did not merely appear as a human being; He truly became human. He experienced hunger, fatigue, sorrow, and pain. This gives Him the unique ability to empathize with the *full range* of human experiences while remaining sinless, providing the perfect and spotless Lamb of God to redeem humanity.

This notion of redemption is central to Jesus' earthly mission. The reason Jesus took on human flesh/form was to redeem mankind from sin. 1 Peter 2:24 tells us, **"He Himself bore our sins in His body on the tree, that we might die to sin and live to righteousness. By His wounds you have been healed."** His physical body became the means by which salvation was made available *to the world*, as He took upon Himself the penalty for sin and provided a way for mankind to be reconciled to the merciful and loving God.

Jesus and the Geography of His Time: The Historical and Cultural Context

To understand the true nature of Jesus, we must also consider the historical and geographical context in which He lived. Jesus was born in Bethlehem in Judea, a region situated in the heart of the ancient Near East. This geographical area, located between the Mediterranean Sea and the Arabian Desert, was far from Europe. The people of this region were Semitic in descent, and Jesus, being a Jew, was part of this group.

The culture, language, and physical features of the people in this area reflected the diverse and often blended ethnic groups that populated the ancient Near East. These people were typically olive-skinned, with dark hair and eyes, consistent with the physical appearance of people from this region today. Matthew 2:1 provides the geographical context, stating, **"Now after Jesus was born in Bethlehem of Judea…"** Jesus was born in a land where people were distinctly Semitic, and the cultural influences in the region were predominantly Middle Eastern (people of color), not European.

Why Jesus Could Not Have Been of European Descent

Given the historical and geographical context of Jesus' life, we can see it is inconceivable that He could have been of European descent. The ancient Near East, where He was born, had a very different racial and ethnic makeup compared to Europe. Jesus, being a Jew from Bethlehem, would have shared the physical features typical of that region — a man of color, quite possibly with dark skin, dark hair, and dark eyes.

Over time, however, especially during the Renaissance and subsequent centuries, European artists and theologians have often depicted Jesus with European features — light skin, blue eyes, and fair/blonde hair. This misrepresentation has persisted, contributing to a Eurocentric view of Jesus that does not align with the geographical and cultural realities of the time. These depictions have not only shaped how many people visualize Jesus but have also reinforced the erroneous idea that Jesus could have been European.

In contrast, the scriptures paint a picture of Jesus as a man who belonged to a specific ethnic group — the Jews — who lived in the region of Judea, at the time part of the occupying Roman Empire, in the Middle East. His physical appearance would have been in line with the people of that region, much like modern-day Jewish, Palestinian, or Arab individuals.

Jesus as the Ultimate Expression of God's Image

Theologically, Jesus is the ultimate expression of God – His Father's image. While humanity was created in God's image (Genesis 1:26-27), the *Edenic Fall* spiritually marred that image along with mankind's physical degradation, and it was only in Jesus Christ that the full, untainted image of God was revealed. Colossians 1:15 refers to Jesus as **"the image of the invisible God, the firstborn of all creation."** He is the perfect reflection of God's nature and character. By taking on human flesh, Jesus demonstrated what it truly means to be created in God's image, perfectly displaying the holiness, love, justice, and truth that His Father intended for humanity.

Through His life, death, and resurrection, Jesus (the second Adam) not only restores the image of God in humanity but also calls all people —

regardless of race, ethnicity, or background — to be conformed to His image. Romans 8:29 says, **"For those whom He foreknew He also predestined to be conformed to the image of His Son…"** In Christ, the restoration of God's image in humanity is made possible. Those who are in Christ are being transformed into His likeness, spiritually renewing the broken image left by the Edenic Fall.

The Ancient Geographical Boundaries and the Impact of Colonialism

To understand the ancient geographical and cultural boundaries of Africa and how they extended into what is now called the Middle East and Asia (the Afro-Asiatic region), one must first recognize that Africa was once more unified—both in cultural identity and regional influence—before external interference and colonization. Historically, its borders were defined by ethnic groups, kingdoms, and trade routes rather than by artificial colonial demarcations. The deep historical and biblical connections between Africa and surrounding regions reveal that Africa played a crucial role in early civilization, commerce, and the development of the Judeo-Christian faith. The imposed divisions that came later were a result of external forces rather than inherent separations.

Ancient Africa stretched beyond what we now recognize as its modern borders, including areas of the Middle East and even parts of Asia. Ancient Egypt, Nubia, and Cush, for example, were central civilizations that bridged Africa and the Middle East. These areas are significant in biblical history as they played key roles in the narratives of Genesis, Exodus, and the surrounding periods.

However, the colonization of Africa in the 19th century resulted in the arbitrary division of these territories, leading to modern borders that ignored historical, ethnic, and cultural divisions. The Suez Canal, which connects the Mediterranean Sea to the Red Sea, has long been a symbol of the strategic importance of the geographical link between Africa and the Middle East. The canal, completed in 1869, made the movement between these regions easier, yet its construction and subsequent geopolitical interests further solidified the boundaries that disregarded ancient historical connections.

A key moment in the reshaping of Africa's borders occurred during the Berlin Conference of 1884-1885, where European powers convened to divide the African continent amongst themselves without regard to the ethnic groups, languages, cultures, or ancient territories that existed. The Berlin Conference is often cited as a foundational moment in the colonization of Africa, where imperial powers imposed their will on a continent, disregarding the rich, interconnected history of African civilizations and the regions adjacent to them, like the Middle East and other parts of Asia. The borders drawn by the colonial powers have led to many modern conflicts within Africa, as they ignored the ancient and ethnic territories that had existed for millennia.

Jesus' Ethnic Identity: A Rich Ancestral Lineage

As we turn to the matter of Jesus' ethnic identity, it is important to address the deep connection between His lineage and the African continent. Jesus' DNA and ancestry trace back to a complex and varied history, which includes individuals whose heritage is tied to Africa, particularly through His maternal side. His earthly ancestors, including figures such as David, Solomon, and Ruth, reveal significant genealogical ties to the broader

Middle Eastern and African regions. In particular, Ruth, a Moabite woman, and Bathsheba, the wife of David, come from regions that are situated in proximity to Africa.

The Moabites, who are believed to have descended from Lot's daughters, lived in a region that bordered Egypt, and Bathsheba's line can be traced back to regions influenced by Egypt and Cush (modern-day Sudan). Through these maternal and paternal connections, Jesus' ethnic identity cannot be divorced from the historical African connection. The geography of His time, from Egypt to Ethiopia, to the ancient lands of Nubia, suggests a lineage deeply rooted in the African world, not simply in terms of skin color but also in terms of culture, history, and religion.

While the specifics of Jesus' physical appearance are not described in the Bible, His ethnic identity as a Jew from the region of Galilee places Him in the context of the peoples who were known to be of darker skin tones, Mediterranean and/or Semitic, rather than European. Jesus, as a man of color in the ancient world, embodied the rich diversity of the region, which was an amalgamation of African, Middle Eastern, and Asian influences, both culturally and genealogically. Let me mention again *we are all one*. And I am convinced that biologically, Jesus embodies **all people**, making Him a man of color and clearly not solely or biologically White.

Race and Cultural Divides in Jesus' Day

One key aspect that must be emphasized is that, during Jesus' lifetime, race, as we understand it today — as a category for social and cultural separation based on skin color — was not a primary issue. While cultural and ethnic divisions existed, they were often rooted in tribal affiliation, religious observance, and geopolitical matters rather than "race." Jesus did not engage in the same racialized thinking that has become so pervasive today. For instance, He interacted with Samaritans (who were seen as culturally and religiously "different" from Jews), Gentiles, and Romans, and He never suggested that one ethnicity was superior to another. His message was clear: all people are created in the image of God, and in Him, there is neither Jew nor Greek, slave nor free, male nor female (Galatians 3:28).

Furthermore, the racialization of humanity was not a concept that Jesus or His contemporaries would have operated in or understood in the modern sense. The ethnic and cultural divides in His day revolved around religious practices and political affiliations, such as the tension between Jews and Gentiles or the Jewish rebellion against Roman rule. Racial and social superiority based on physical appearance or skin color was not central to Jesus' ministry or teachings. His focus was on the heart and spiritual redemption, not on the corrupt flesh that presently clothe humanity, which He emphasized would one day be transformed (1 Corinthians 15:52-54).

Jesus, therefore, did not see ethnic distinctions or tribal affiliations as barriers to salvation. The flesh — and, by extension, one's ethnicity — was temporary, and the ultimate concern for Jesus was the spiritual condition of the soul. This aligns with His message of eternal life and spiritual renewal. Jesus did not advocate for ethnic or cultural superiority; rather, He came to redeem humanity from sin and show that all men, women, and children, regardless of ethnicity or race, have equal value before God.

Closing Remarks of Chapter 3

In Chapter 3, we journeyed through the scientific evidence that traces humanity's origins to Africa, where the genetic and mitochondrial studies confirm that all humans share common ancestors from this continent. The mitochondrial Eve and the Y-chromosomal studies provide compelling proof that, genetically speaking, all of humanity is linked to Africa. These findings, while fascinating, not only confirm our shared biological lineage but also challenge modern constructs of race that have historically been used to divide and oppress. These studies emphasize our unity as the children of one Creator, regardless of physical or ethnic differences. Humanity's genetic connection transcends artificial racial categories and should lead to a deeper recognition of our common humanity.

As we explored the geographical and cultural boundaries of the ancient world, we reflected on how the colonial imposition of borders, particularly the carving up of Africa by European powers during the Berlin Conference, fractured the historical, ethnic, and cultural unity that once existed across Africa, the Middle East, and Asia. This imposed fragmentation created enduring divisions that continue to shape geopolitical tensions in our world today. The historical context of the Suez Canal and how the ancient world of Africa and the Middle East interacted also provides valuable insight into the broader cultural and spiritual history of these regions and their connection to the biblical narrative.

Turning our focus to the ethnic identity of Jesus Christ, we recognized that the Savior, born in the Middle East, was not a European figure, but one whose lineage was rooted in the ethnic and cultural diversity of the ancient world. His lineage, both through His earthly mother, Mary and His genealogical descent, was deeply tied to the people of that region, and through Biblical records, we see connections to various ethnic groups, including those of African descent. This understanding challenges the European-centered depictions of Christ and places Him firmly within the historical and ethnic context of His time.

More importantly, Jesus' ministry was not concerned with the racial or cultural divisions that would later plague humanity. In His time, cultural divisions were more about religious and political allegiances, not the skin color and/or ethnicity that divides us today. Jesus transcended these divisions, focusing instead on the condition of the heart and the need for redemption. He did not see one race or ethnicity as superior to another, as many have misinterpreted over the centuries. His mission was to bring ***all people into a right relationship with God, breaking down the walls of hostility that sin had erected between us.***

Jesus also taught that the fallen human body, while sacred as a creation of God, is ultimately temporal and will be transformed in the resurrection. The distinctions of race and culture, though meaningful in the temporal world, do not define our eternal worth. Our true identity is found in Christ, who came to redeem all of humanity and restore us to our original purpose — to reflect God's image and live in unity with one another.

In closing, this chapter has underscored the importance of understanding our shared origins, the unifying truth of our creation in God's image, and how Jesus' work offers the key to overcoming divisions. While modern notions of race have caused significant harm and division, the gospel message remains clear: our true identity is not defined by the flesh, but by the spirit. In Christ, there is no Jew nor Greek, slave nor free, male nor female — we are all one in Him. This profound truth should transform how we view ourselves and one another, reminding us that in Christ, all are equal, and all are beloved of God, but only the redeemed of Jesus are the true children of God.

CHAPTER 4

The War on Identity: Psychological and Spiritual Warfare

The Bible is very clear that no engraved images were to be made of God. This commandment, explicitly given in Exodus 20:4,5, was meant to prevent idolatry and the misrepresentation of the divine nature of God. Throughout Israel's history, God repeatedly warned His people against crafting any physical representation of Him, knowing that human attempts to depict the divine would fall short and lead to false worship. What is remarkable, then, is that during the life of Christ, there is no record of anyone attempting to make an image of Him. Unlike rulers, emperors, or prominent figures of His time whose likenesses were often immortalized in statues and paintings, Jesus left no physical portrait behind; even so, He made it clear that His Kingdom was not of this world. His mission was not to establish a physical identity to be memorialized in artwork, but to reveal the Father – God who is the Supreme Creator and Spirit-being and to redeem humanity through His life, death, and resurrection.

Nevertheless, in later centuries, as Christianity spread, men took it upon themselves, against the command of God, to depict Jesus – the Unique Son of God visually, despite the clear Biblical command against doing so.

Colonizers and others who sought to shape history to favor their narrative, culture and likeness produced images of a white, European-looking Jesus after their likeness. These paintings and sculptures, which depict Jesus with pale skin, light-colored eyes, and European-style hair, became the dominant portrayal of Christ in Western traditions. These images are not only historically and biblically inaccurate, but they have also caused great confusion and even rejection of Jesus, particularly among those who recognize their falsehood.

Perhaps you, like many others, have encountered these misleading images—whether in churches, homes, religious literature or elsewhere. These portrayals have shaped the way generations have perceived Jesus, embedding a false representation into Christian tradition. Yet, Scripture gives no physical description of Jesus during His earthly ministry. The only reference to His appearance is found in Isaiah 53:2, which emphasizes that there was nothing outwardly striking about Him that would attract people to Him. Furthermore, Revelation 1:14-15, often mistakenly cited as a literal description of Christ, is widely understood by theologians as symbolic, portraying His divine majesty rather than His earthly features.

However, the Roman Catholic Church, along with various Orthodox churches and some Protestant traditions, has embraced religious imagery, including depictions of Jesus and Mary in paintings, sculptures, and stained glass. The Vatican (RCC), for instance, is filled with countless images of Christ, many of which depict Him in a European likeness. Statues of Mary, often adorned and venerated, are also prominently displayed. In contrast, Orthodox churches generally use icons, focusing more on two-dimensional depictions. Such representations directly contradict the Biblical prohibition against making images of God – hence Jesus (Deuteronomy 4:15-16), yet they persist under the justification of aiding worship and devotion. This practice, however, has led many into idolatry, as people pray before these images, attributing to them a sacred significance that God never ordained.

The Satanic Influence Behind Idolatry

Throughout the Bible, one of the greatest evils committed by humanity has been the crafting and worship of images that are presumed to represent God or false gods. The Israelites, despite being given direct commands against idolatry, frequently fell into the sin of making idols. One of the most notorious examples is found in Exodus 32, where they fashioned the golden calf, declaring it to be their god. This was not merely an act of misguided worship; it was influenced by demonic deception.

Idolatry is never just about the fashioning of wood, stone, or metal as a god or such things being idolized. The spiritual reality behind it is demonic influence. In Psalm 106:36-37, Scripture explicitly states that the Israelites' idol worship led them to sacrifice their sons and daughters to demons. Likewise, 1 Corinthians 10:20 warns that those who worship idols are actually offering sacrifices to demons. This reveals that behind every false image and/or counterfeit image of God, including false depictions of Jesus, there lurks a satanic agenda—one that seeks to distort the truth, deceive people, and draw them away from the living God and one another.

Even today, many cultures continue to create images as their gods or for their gods, which are spirit entities. However, knowingly or not, behind these creations and idol worship, actually active in the unseen realm, are dark or wicked *fallen* or *rebellious* spirits. All heavenly beings, angels or spirit beings are elohim. Yet, God alone – Yahweh, is the eternal or *Self-existent Sovereign Elohim and Creator of all*. As suggested in some traditions, these images are not mere artistic expressions but are believed to house or represent spiritual forces. This is why God's command remains unchanged—He is not to be represented by any image. No human depiction can ever capture His essence, and every attempt to do so opens the door to spiritual deception.

The Symbolic Meaning of Jesus' Image in Revelation 1:14-15

While many have tried to use Revelation 1:14-15 as proof of Jesus' physical features, a deeper biblical study reveals that these descriptions are highly symbolic. The white hair is not about ethnicity but represents His eternal existence and divine wisdom. In Daniel 7:9, God Himself, the **"Ancient of Days,"** is described as having hair **"white like wool,"** signifying purity, holiness, and the infinite wisdom of God. This same imagery is applied to Christ, affirming His divinity and His eternal nature.

His eyes, like a flame of fire, speak of His omniscience and penetrating judgment. Fire in the Bible often represents purification and divine judgment (Malachi 3:2-3, 1 Corinthians 3:13-15). The fiery eyes of Christ symbolize His ability to see all things and to judge righteously. No one can hide from His gaze, for He searches the hearts and minds of all people (Revelation 2:23).

His feet like fine brass, as if refined in a furnace, symbolize strength, stability, and divine authority. In biblical imagery, brass (or bronze) is associated with judgment and endurance. The bronze serpent in Numbers 21:9 and the bronze altar in the Tabernacle (Exodus 27:1-2) were symbols of God's judgment upon sin. Christ's feet, refined as in a furnace, represent His complete triumph over sin, suffering, and judgment.

Thus, Revelation 1:14-15 does not give us a physical picture of Jesus but rather a spiritual revelation of His divine attributes. To reduce this passage to a racial or ethnic description misses the entire point. Christ is the eternal, All-seeing, All-judging King whose wisdom, purity, and authority extend beyond any human category of race or physical form.

No Image Can Contain the True Christ

The consequences of these misrepresentations have been far-reaching. For many, the Eurocentric portrayal of Jesus has become a stumbling block, reinforcing the false notion that Christianity is a "white man's religion." This has led some to reject the faith altogether, believing that it was constructed to serve European interests. However, the true Christ transcends race, culture, and human depiction. God is not concerned with outward appearance but with the heart (1 Samuel 16:7). Jesus came to redeem all people—not one ethnicity or nation, but all who believe in Him, for **"from one man, He made all the nations"** (Acts 17:26).

The Bible is clear—no images of Christ should be made. Whether intended as a cultural expression, an artistic rendering, or a devotional aid, all attempts to depict Jesus violate God's command. They reduce the infinite and eternal Son of God to a finite, human-made representation that inevitably distorts who He truly is. The danger is not merely in the inaccuracy of these images but in the false perceptions and theological errors they create. No image can ever capture the fullness of Christ, and attempting to do so only distracts from His true nature and mission.

As this book continues, we will build upon the reality of Christ beyond human distortion. The misrepresentations of Jesus' image have played a significant role in shaping societies, reinforcing biases, and even being weaponized for political and social control. However, the real Jesus—the eternal Word taking on flesh as a covering—can only be known through the truth of Scripture and the power of the indwelling Holy Spirit. It is only by looking to the unseen Christ through faith, rather than to human-crafted images, that we come to truly know Him.

This aspect of the chapter is crucial because it highlights not only the spiritual warfare involved in distorting the image of Christ but also the intentional psychological warfare waged against African Americans and other oppressed peoples. The historical use of a whitewashed Jesus was not merely or always an innocent artistic rendering—it was Psy-Ops (psychological operation and warfare) designed to manipulate and control the minds of those who were enslaved and subjugated. Colonizers, many of whom claimed to be Christians, knew exactly what they were doing when they reimagined Christ in their own image and presented this false depiction to the people they sought to dominate or the minds of others they desired to direct.

By enforcing an image of Jesus as European-looking, with pale skin, blond hair, and blue eyes, these colonizers sought to embed a sense of inferiority in the minds of enslaved Africans and other non-white groups. The strategy was simple yet devastating: if God Himself was depicted as White, then whiteness became synonymous with divinity, authority, and superiority. In contrast, darker-skinned people, particularly those of African descent, were subtly and even overtly conditioned to believe that they were inferior, unworthy, or even cursed. This was not just an act of cultural distortion—it was a weaponized lie designed to break the spirit and faith or belief systems of an entire people.

The Enduring Presence of Eurocentric Jesus

As mentioned, images of a white Jesus have appeared in churches, homes, and religious literature for centuries. These depictions were not only found in America but were aggressively spread across the world through colonization and missionary efforts. Even today, in some predominantly "Black churches," paintings of a European-looking Christ can still be found. Many Believers, without realizing it, have internalized this image, making it difficult for them to truly connect with the historical and Biblical Jesus.

My personal experience at a predominantly "White church" reinforced this reality for me in a profound and bothersome way. My wife and I were warmly welcomed by the congregation—from the moment we arrived until the time we left. There was no hostility, no sense of exclusion. We genuinely felt welcomed as fellow Believers in Christ. However, what we witnessed during the service left us deeply disturbed.

This visit occurred during the Christmas season, a time when churches traditionally focus on celebrating the birth of Christ. One of the pastors was giving a presentation about Christmas, which included visual aids to help convey his message. As we sat and listened, it became clear that he had chosen to depict Jesus and other biblical figures as Eurocentric. He displayed images of white, blond-haired, blue-eyed figures, reinforcing the very falsehood that has been used for centuries to mislead people about Jesus' true identity. I will also mention the fact that Caucasians also depict angels as being white. This, too, is concerning!

In this modern era, when so much historical and Biblical scholarship has made it clear that Jesus was not a white man, it was deeply troubling to see this misrepresentation still being promoted. While I could understand that older generations may have been taught these images without question, there is no excuse today. The truth is widely available, and churches have a responsibility to correct these errors, especially when they have contributed to so much spiritual and psychological damage.

Confronting the Issue Directly

After much thought, I decided to address this issue directly with the lead pastor through an email. In my message, I respectfully expressed my concerns, emphasizing that both he and I knew that, culturally, Jesus was not a white man. I pointed out that erroneous and misleading depictions of Christ have caused many African Americans to reject Christianity altogether because they have been conditioned to associate Him with their oppressors. I urged him to reconsider the images that the church presents and to acknowledge the harm that such misrepresentations have caused.

To my utter surprise, the pastor agreed with me. He acknowledged that the depiction of Jesus as a white man was inaccurate, and he admitted that he understood how this could be a stumbling block for many people, particularly in the Black community. While I do not know whether the church has taken active steps to correct this issue, the fact that he was willing to listen and acknowledge the problem was significant and greatly appreciated.

The Need for Truth in the Church

This experience serves as a reminder that churches must be intentional about presenting biblical truth—not cultural distortions. It is not enough to simply preach the gospel while allowing false images to persist. The visual representations that churches display shape the way people understand God, and if those images are false, they contribute to false theology, racial bias, and division within the body of Christ, if not the utter rejection of Him.

Furthermore, this is not just about race—it is about honoring God's command. As previously stated, Exodus 20:4-5 makes it clear that we are not to create any images of God. The Catholic Church, as well as various Orthodox and Protestant traditions, have disregarded this command, filling their places of worship with images of Jesus and Mary. Whether these images are European, African, or any other ethnicity, they are still human attempts to depict the divine, which is strictly forbidden by Scripture or God Himself.

Idolatry is not simply about bowing to statues—it is about misrepresenting God, allowing false images to shape our understanding of Him. This is why Satan has worked tirelessly to distort the image of Christ—because he knows that if people believe in a false representation of Christ, they will struggle to truly connect with the real Christ.

Breaking the Chains of Psychological Warfare

The weaponization of Jesus' image has been one of the most effective tools used against African Americans and other oppressed people. But the truth sets us free (John 8:32). It is time for churches, pastors, and Believers to reject false representations and embrace the true, living Christ—the One who is beyond race, beyond culture, and beyond human manipulation.

Having mentioned the experience that I had at the church, there are two other experiences that I want to share with you regarding one's perception of whiteness and another person's remaining warped ideology with regard to racism.

The first individual I will speak of was actually a family member—an older member of the family, perhaps in his late 70s or early 80s at the time. Despite having experienced racism firsthand in his youth, he nevertheless embraced the image of a white Jesus. As an elder church leader, he was responsible for putting together a monthly devotional brochure, which contained valuable Biblical insights and reflections. However, one troubling aspect of this publication was the image that consistently adorned its cover—an unmistakable depiction of a white Jesus, not unlike the images often seen in churches and homes.

Recognizing the theological, historical, and geographical inaccuracies of this portrayal, I felt compelled to address it. I approached him with the truth, explaining how such images misrepresent Christ and stand in direct opposition to Scripture. I laid out the facts—both biblically and logically—hoping he would recognize the error and make a necessary correction. However, rather than receiving my words with understanding, he responded in a way that exposed a deeper issue at play. He told me that when he prayed on the matter, this was what God had told him to do.

This response was alarming. It was not merely an issue of personal preference or cultural tradition—it was evidence of spiritual and psychological warfare. How is it that an otherwise devout man, who had dedicated his life to serving in the church, could be so deeply entrenched in this deception? How had the psychological conditioning been so effective that he genuinely believed God had instructed him to perpetuate an image of Christ that was historically and biblically false?

Then, there was another individual—an older white woman (Ms Trudy) in her mid-to-late 70s at the time. She and I were in a training class together through our respective churches. Although we came from different backgrounds, I thought highly of her and considered her a sister in Christ. Despite the generational and "racial" divide, I saw her as someone with whom I could build a lasting connection. During our opening class introduction, Ms. Trudy, while providing information about herself, mentioned that her husband had recently passed. No one in the class of about 20 people expressed sympathy towards Ms. Trudy. I was the last person to introduce myself. Before doing so, I recognized Ms. Trudy's loss. I stated to the class that Ms. Trudy was certainly grieving the passing of her husband and that we should be in prayer for her. For reasons unknown to me at the time, I was drawn towards Ms. Trudy.

Two weeks later, as the class was coming to an end, I expressed my desire to maintain our relationship beyond the course. I gave her my phone number and told her I would love to stay in touch. She received my contact information, but she said nothing in response. I did not think much of it at the time. However, a couple of days later, she called me. There was urgency in her voicemail, as if something pressing had weighed heavily on her heart. She insisted that we meet and talk.

When I arrived at her home, I was not invited inside. Instead, we sat on the porch, and on that beautiful day, she revealed to me something I had not anticipated. She looked me in the eyes and said, "When you told me you wanted to stay in touch with me, my first thought was, 'You are out of place.'"

Her words caught me completely off guard. "You are out of place."

This was not merely an offhand comment. This was a phrase steeped in history—a phrase Black Men and Women had heard for generations whenever they stepped beyond the boundaries imposed upon them by a racist society. It was a phrase used to remind African Americans "to know their place." And here she was, admitting that this was her immediate reaction to my simple offer of friendship.

She went on to explain that my words had forced her to confront her "own bigotry"—something she had not even realized remained within her. She recounted her childhood experiences as a white girl growing up in segregation and how she was raised to see the world through a lens that kept blacks and whites separate. She recalled a particular incident from her youth when her family had taken a trip to the beach. She had wanted their Black Housekeeper—the woman who had cared for her and nurtured her—to join them on the sand. But she was quickly informed that the beach was for white people only, and that their Black Nanny could not step foot on it.

It was at that moment of me reaching out to her as a friend that she experienced how deeply ingrained these racial barriers had been in her upbringing. Although, as a child, she was unable to comprehend the devilish depth and division of the construct of race, which had become engraved in her mind through conditioning – Psy-Ops. She admitted that my words had forced her to wrestle with prejudices she had carried for decades—prejudices that had been so deeply embedded in her psyche that she had not even recognized them as such. Clearly, for years, her involvement with Blacks had been little to none.

Again, I return to the matter of psychological warfare. How many people, both Black and White, have been unknowingly conditioned by the systems and images that have been perpetuated for centuries? How many African Americans have been taught—either explicitly or subconsciously—that the white Jesus is their Savior, while at the same time being treated as less than by the very people – whites who, without reservation, worship Him. Even so, while some Blacks continue to embrace the **Great lie** that they are/were inferior and even cursed. How many white Christians have been raised to see themselves as inherently superior, not realizing that these ideas were instilled in them by a society that was more concerned with maintaining power than with upholding the true gospel of Christ?

The battle against false imagery is not just about correcting artistic misrepresentations—it is about breaking chains. It is about undoing centuries of conditioning that have distorted the way people see Christ and, in turn, the way they see themselves and each other.

It is only when we embrace Christ in Spirit and in Truth that these lies can be broken.

The War on Identity

The psychological assaults did not stop there. Colonizers, driven by demonic influences, their own lust and desire to maintain power, dominance, and control, created a system that entrenched white superiority at every level. I must emphasize this was not merely a social or political structure; it was also deeply spiritual in nature, and yet, psychological warfare utilized by these human agents under the influence and even many, spiritual possession of the forces of darkness. These tactics were deliberate and aimed at breaking the spirit and beliefs of those they sought to subjugate, particularly Africans, who were enslaved and subjected to inhumane conditions, both physically and psychologically.

In addition to the divisions created between whites and blacks, the same system, through psychological conditioning, was also designed to infiltrate

Black communities, even among Black families themselves. During slavery, lighter-skinned blacks, often the result of sexual relations—or even rape—between slave owners and enslaved women, were viewed as superior to darker-skinned blacks. This division was fostered by the very same colonizers who used skin color to create hierarchies or favor within the African American community. The darker the skin, the more degraded and inferior one was perceived to be. This internalized racism has persisted in various forms, causing division and, for many, self-loathing within the African American community, and the effects continue to be felt today.

Moreover, this division wasn't limited to the United States; European countries were equally complicit in spreading the ideology of racial superiority. European textbooks, school curriculums, and various other media were strategically designed to instill the belief that Black people were inferior to whites. The school curriculum and systems portrayed Africans and their cultures as primitive, backward, and savage. I tell you, these depictions were not just incidental; they were intentionally crafted to reinforce the ideological framework of so-called European superiority, ensuring that the children of European nations would grow up believing in their fanciful inherent superiority over the African people; as for "Blacks," many viewing themselves as less than or inferior.

This educational indoctrination was not confined to the schools. The media, literature, and art of the time portrayed Black people as ignorant and less than human, further embedding these racist beliefs in the collective psyche of both the colonizers and the colonized. In Britain, France, Spain, and other colonial powers, this racial hierarchy was woven into every aspect of life. Not only were the colonizers seen as superior, but their dominance was justified through a pseudo-scientific rationale, claiming that non-Europeans were biologically and intellectually inferior. This ideological framework justified the inhumane treatment of enslaved Africans and the systematic exploitation of their free labor.

One of the most infamous expressions of psychological warfare was allegedly expressed within the "Willie Lynch Letter," a document purportedly written in the 18th century that provided instructions for dividing and controlling enslaved Africans. Although *there is debate about its authenticity*, the methods outlined in the letter *reflect the tactics that were <u>widely</u> used during the slavery era to keep African people divided and in their place.* The alleged letter instructed slave owners to create divisions among the enslaved based on factors like skin color, age, and even gender, ensuring that they would remain divided and unable to unite against their oppressors. These strategies were meant to create distrust, resentment, and competition among the enslaved, making them less likely to rebel or organize. The results were devastating and long-lasting, perpetuating the psychological and emotional scars of slavery for generations.

This practice of psychological warfare did not end with the abolition of slavery. The impact of this deep division instilled in the psyche of many continued and continues well into the 20th and 21st centuries. African Americans continue to face systemic racism, perpetuated not only through laws and policies but also through deeply ingrained social and psychological structures designed to perpetuate the *Great Lie*. The myth of white superiority has not been dismantled, and many of the tactics used to divide the African American community continue to be effective. The same racial divisions—light-skinned versus dark-skinned—persist in the minds of some "Blacks," further complicating the struggle for unity and equality in-house and societally.

And so, the psychological warfare and spiritual warfare waged during the time of colonization and slavery continue to shape the identity and experience of African Americans. From the misrepresentation of Jesus as a white man to the continued perpetuation of racial stereotypes, the battle for identity is far from over. As we continue to reflect on these issues, it's important to recognize that they are not just remnants of history but active, ongoing struggles that require spiritual and psychological healing.

Conclusion of Chapter Four: The War on Identity

In this chapter, we have examined the layers of warfare—psychological, spiritual, or ideological—that have been waged throughout history to shape the identity of African Americans and other marginalized peoples. This war has been fought not just through the exploitation of bodies but also through the strategic manipulation of minds or, hearts, and souls. From the moment of colonization and the advent of slavery, the *Great lie* of white superiority was spread and deeply embedded within the social, political, and religious structures of society. These systems sought to dehumanize, degrade, and divide, ensuring that the victims of oppression were kept spiritually and psychologically enslaved, even after the physical chains were broken.

The false images of God, the Son–Jesus, and the depiction of a white Jesus have been one of the most potent tools in this psychological and spiritual warfare. The Bible is very clear that no images were to be made of God (Exodus 20:4-5), yet throughout colonial history and presently, the image of a white Jesus has been used to reinforce the *Great lie* of white superiority. The image of Christ as white continues to resonate deeply in Western culture, making it difficult for many, particularly African Americans, to see Christ as their Savior in an authentic and personal way.

This image distorts not only the true identity of Christ but also the identity of those who are called to be His followers. It is a theological deception that continues to impact countless individuals.

Furthermore, the internal divisions within the African American community—fueled by colorism and the legacy of slavery—remain a significant point of struggle. Lighter-skinned blacks, often the result of slave owners' exploitation of black women, were historically given privileges over their darker-skinned counterparts. This division, rooted in the demonic system of slavery, has lingered in the minds of many within the African American community. The skin color divide perpetuates self-hate and impedes unity, continuing to work against efforts to heal the psychological wounds inflicted by centuries of systemic racism.

The psychological effects of colonization and slavery were not limited to the subjugated people. The dominant European cultures that perpetuated these ideologies have continued to transmit these racist views through textbooks, educational curriculums, and media. European nations taught their children to believe in the inherent superiority of the white race while simultaneously painting black people as inferior, savage, and subhuman. This pervasive indoctrination became the foundation of white supremacy, which was justified under the guise of scientific racism and religious teachings.

The questionable "Willie Lynch Letter" stands as one of the most infamous examples of this effort to control and divide. This unauthenticated letter's instructions for turning black people against each other—creating distrust, resentment, and competition—served as a blueprint for ensuring that African Americans would never unite against their oppressors. Although the letter's authenticity is debated, its contents reflect the *real practices* of slavery and the deep spiritual and psychological manipulation used to enforce racial hierarchy.

Even today, the psychological warfare and spiritual warfare waged during the time of colonization and slavery continue to shape the identity and experience of many African Americans. From the perpetuation of racial stereotypes to the continued misrepresentation of Christ, the battle for identity is ongoing. These forces continue to distort and confuse the true identity of many African Americans and others, keeping many from fully embracing their worth and dignity as imagers and even children of God. But there is hope. Through Christ, there is liberation from these lies, and through spiritual and psychological healing, African Americans—and all people—can reclaim their true identity. This is the victory promised to us, one that transcends the false images and lies of the past.

As we move forward, we must confront these lies, reject the false teachings that have divided us, and rebuild an understanding of ourselves that is rooted in truth. Only then can we find the strength to heal from the wounds of the past and walk in the freedom that Christ offers. The war on identity is not just a battle for history, but for the present and future of all people. By reclaiming our true identity in Christ, we can overcome the spiritual and psychological warfare that has been waged for so long.

Although the following letter, for good reasons, has been called into question by scholars and historians, nevertheless, it provides insight into the mentality and methods utilized by many antebellum enslavers.

"Willie Lynch letter:"

"The Making of a Slave This speech was delivered by Willie Lynch on the bank of the James River in the colony of Virginia in 1712. Lynch was a British slave owner in the West Indies. He was invited to the colony of Virginia in 1712 to teach his methods to slave owners there. The term "lynching" is derived from his last name. [beginning of the Willie Lynch Letter] Greetings, Gentlemen. I greet you here on the bank of the James River in the year of our Lord one thousand seven hundred and twelve. First, I shall thank you, the gentlemen of the Colony of Virginia, for bringing me here. I am here to help you solve some of your problems with slaves. Your invitation reached me on my modest plantation in the West Indies, where I have experimented with some of the newest, and still the oldest, methods for control of slaves. Ancient Rome would envy us if my program is implemented. As our boat sailed south on the James River, named for our illustrious King, whose version of the Bible we cherish, I saw enough to know that your problem is not unique. While Rome used cords of wood as crosses for standing human bodies along its highways in great numbers, you are here using the tree and the rope on occasions. I caught the whiff of a dead slave hanging from a tree, a couple miles back. You are not only losing valuable stock by hangings, you are having uprisings, slaves are running away, your crops are sometimes left in the fields too long for maximum profit, you suffer occasional fires, your animals are killed. Gentlemen, you know what your problems are; I do not need to elaborate. I am not here to enumerate your problems, I am here to introduce you to a method of solving them. In my bag here, I HAVE A FULL PROOF METHOD FOR CONTROLLING YOUR BLACK SLAVES. I guarantee every one of you that, if installed correctly, IT WILL CONTROL THE SLAVES FOR AT LEAST 300 HUNDREDS YEARS.

My method is simple. Any member of your family or your overseer can use it. I HAVE OUTLINED A NUMBER OF DIFFERENCES AMONG THE SLAVES; AND I TAKE THESE DIFFERENCES AND MAKE THEM BIGGER. I USE FEAR, DISTRUST AND ENVY FOR CONTROL PURPOSES. These methods have worked on my modest plantation in the West Indies and it will work throughout the South. Take this simple little list of differences and think about them. On top of my list is "AGE," but it's there only because it starts with an "a." The second is "COLOR" or shade. There is INTELLIGENCE, SIZE, SEX, SIZES OF PLANTATIONS, STATUS on plantations, ATTITUDE of owners, whether the slaves live in the valley, on a hill, East, West, North, South, have fine hair, course hair, or is tall or short. Now that you have a list of differences, I shall give you an outline of action, but before that, I shall assure you that DISTRUST IS STRONGER THAN TRUST AND ENVY STRONGER THAN ADULATION, RESPECT OR ADMIRATION. The Black slaves after receiving this indoctrination shall carry on and will become self-refueling and self-generating for HUNDREDS of years, maybe THOUSANDS. Don't forget, you must pitch the OLD black male vs. the YOUNG black male, and the YOUNG black male against the OLD black male. You must use the DARK skin slaves vs. the LIGHT skin slaves, and the LIGHT skin slaves vs. the DARK skin slaves. You must use the FEMALE vs. the MALE, and the MALE vs. the FEMALE. You must also have white servants and overseers [who] distrust all Blacks. But it is NECESSARY THAT YOUR SLAVES TRUST AND DEPEND ON US. THEY MUST LOVE, RESPECT AND TRUST ONLY US. Gentlemen, these kits are your keys to control. Use them. Have your wives and children use them, never miss an opportunity. IF USED INTENSELY FOR ONE YEAR, THE SLAVES THEMSELVES WILL REMAIN PERPETUALLY DISTRUSTFUL.

Thank you gentlemen." LET'S MAKE A SLAVE It was the interest and business of slave holders to study human nature, and the slave nature in particular, with a view to practical results. I and many of them attained astonishing proficiency in this direction. They had to deal not with earth, wood and stone, but with men and, by every regard, they had for their own safety and prosperity they needed to know the material on which they were to work, conscious of the injustice and wrong they were every hour perpetuating and knowing what they themselves would do. Were they the victims of such wrongs? They were constantly looking for the first signs of the dreaded retribution. They watched therefore with skilled and practiced eyes, and learned to read with great accuracy, the state of mind and heart of the slave, through his sable face. Unusual sobriety, apparent abstractions, sullenness and indifference indeed, any mood out of the common was afforded ground for suspicion and inquiry. Frederick Douglas LET'S MAKE A SLAVE is a study of the scientific process of man-breaking and slave-making. It describes the rationale and results of the Anglo Saxons' ideas and methods of insuring the master/slave relationship. LET'S MAKE A SLAVE "The Original and Development of a Social Being Called 'The Negro.'" Let us make a slave. What do we need? First of all, we need a black nigger man, a pregnant nigger woman and her baby nigger boy. Second, we will use the same basic principle that we use in breaking a horse, combined with some more sustaining factors. What we do with horses is that we break them from one form of life to another; that is, we reduce them from their natural state in nature. Whereas nature provides them with the natural capacity to take care of their offspring, we break that natural string of independence from them and thereby create a dependency status, so that we may be able to get from them useful production for our business and pleasure. CARDINAL PRINCIPLES FOR MAKING A NEGRO For fear that our future generations may not understand the principles of breaking both of the beast together, the nigger and the horse. We understand that short range planning economics results in periodic economic chaos; so that to avoid turmoil in the economy, it requires us to have breadth and depth in long range comprehensive planning, articulating both skill sharp perceptions. We lay down the following principles for long range comprehensive economic planning. Both horse and niggers [are] no good to the economy in the wild or natural state. Both must be BROKEN and TIED together for orderly production. For orderly future, special and particular attention must be paid to the FEMALE and the YOUNGEST offspring. Both must be CROSSBRED to produce a variety and division of labor. Both must be taught to respond to a peculiar new LANGUAGE. Psychological and physical instruction of CONTAINMENT must be created for both. We hold the six cardinal principles as truth to be self-evident, based upon following the discourse concerning the economics of breaking and tying the horse and the nigger together, all inclusive of the six principles laid down above. NOTE: Neither principle alone will suffice for good economics. All principles must be employed for orderly good of the nation. Accordingly, both a wild horse and a wild or natur[al] nigger is dangerous even if captured, for they will have the tendency to seek their customary freedom and, in doing so, might kill you in your sleep. You cannot rest. They sleep while you are awake, and are awake while you are asleep. They are DANGEROUS near the family house and it requires too much labor to watch them away from the house. Above all, you cannot get them to work in this natural state. Hence, both the horse and the nigger must be broken; that is breaking them from one form of mental life to another. KEEP THE BODY, TAKE THE MIND! In other words, break the will to resist. Now the breaking process is the same for both the horse and the nigger, only slightly varying in degrees. But, as we said before, there is an art in long range economic planning. YOU MUST KEEP YOUR

EYE AND THOUGHTS ON THE FEMALE and the OFFSPRING of the horse and the nigger. A brief discourse in offspring development will shed light on the key to sound economic principles. Pay little attention to the generation of original breaking, but CONCENTRATE ON FUTURE GENERATION. Therefore, if you break the FEMALE mother, she will BREAK the offspring in its early years of development; and when the offspring is old enough to work, she will deliver it up to you, for her normal female protective tendencies will have been lost in the original breaking process. For example, take the case of the wild stud horse, a female horse and an already infant horse and compare the breaking process with two captured nigger males in their natural state, a pregnant nigger woman with her infant offspring. Take the stud horse, break him for limited containment. Completely break the female horse until she becomes very gentle, whereas you or anybody can ride her in her comfort. Breed the mare and the stud until you have the desired offspring. Then, you can turn the stud to freedom until you need him again. Train the female horse whereby she will eat out of your hand, and she will in turn train the infant horse to eat out of your hand, also. When it comes to breaking the uncivilized nigger, use the same process, but vary the degree and step up the pressure, so as to do a complete reversal of the mind. Take the meanest and most restless nigger, strip him of his clothes in front of the remaining male niggers, the female, and the nigger infant, tar and feather him, tie each leg to a different horse faced in opposite directions, set him afire and beat both horses to pull him apart in front of the remaining niggers. The next step is to take a bullwhip and beat the remaining nigger males to the point of death, in front of the female and the infant. Don't kill him, but PUT THE FEAR OF GOD IN HIM, for he can be useful for future breeding. THE BREAKING PROCESS OF THE AFRICAN WOMAN Take the female and run a series of tests on her to see if she will submit to your desires willingly. Test her in every way, because she is the most important factor for good economics. If she shows any sign of resistance in submitting completely to your will, do not hesitate to use the bullwhip on her to extract that last bit of [b----] out of her. Take care not to kill her, for in doing so, you spoil good economics. When in complete submission, she will train her offsprings in the early years to submit to labor when they become of age. Understanding is the best thing. Therefore, we shall go deeper into this area of the subject matter concerning what we have produced here in this breaking process of the female nigger. We have reversed the relationship; in her natural uncivilized state, she would have a strong dependency on the uncivilized nigger male, and she would have a limited protective tendency toward her independent male offspring and would raise male offsprings to be dependent like her. Nature had provided for this type of balance. We reversed nature by burning and pulling a civilized nigger apart and bullwhipping the other to the point of death, all in her presence. By her being left alone, unprotected, with the MALE IMAGE DESTROYED, the ordeal caused her to move from her psychologically dependent state to a frozen, independent state. In this frozen, psychological state of independence, she will raise her MALE and female offspring in reversed roles. For FEAR of the young male's life, she will psychologically train him to be MENTALLY WEAK and DEPENDENT, but PHYSICALLY STRONG. Because she has become psychologically independent, she will train her FEMALE offsprings to be psychologically independent. What have you got? You've got the nigger WOMAN OUT FRONT AND THE nigger MAN BEHIND AND SCARED. This is a perfect situation of sound sleep and economics. Before the breaking process, we had to be alertly on guard at all times. Now, we can sleep soundly, for out of frozen fear his woman stands guard for us. He cannot get past her early slave molding process. He is a good tool, now ready to be tied to the horse at a tender age. By the time a nigger boy reaches the age of sixteen, he is soundly broken in and ready for a long life of sound and efficient work and the reproduction of a unit of good labor force. Continually through the breaking of uncivilized savage niggers, by throwing the nigger female savage into a frozen psychological state of independence, by killing the protective male image, and by creating a submissive dependent mind of the nigger male slave, we have created an orbiting cycle that turns on its own axis forever, unless a phenomenon occurs and re-shifts the position of the male and female slaves. We show what we mean by example. Take the case of the two economic slave units and examine them close. THE NEGRO MARRIAGE We breed two nigger males with two nigger females. Then, we take the nigger male away from them and keep them moving and working. Say one nigger female bears a nigger female and the other bears a nigger male; both nigger females—being without influence of the nigger male image, frozen with a independent psychology—will raise their offspring into reverse positions. The one with the female offspring will teach her to be like herself, independent and negotiable (we negotiate with her, through her, by her, negotiates her at will). The one with the nigger male offspring, she being frozen subconscious fear for his life, will raise him to be mentally dependent and weak, but physically strong; in other words, body over mind. Now, in a few years when these two offsprings become fertile for early reproduction, we will mate and breed them and continue the cycle. That is good, sound and long range comprehensive planning. WARNING: POSSIBLE INTERLOPING NEGATIVES Earlier, we talked about the non-economic good of the horse and the nigger in their wild or natural state; we talked out the principle of breaking and tying them together for orderly production. Furthermore, we talked about paying particular attention to the female savage and her offspring for orderly future

81

planning, then more recently we stated that, by reversing the positions of the male and female savages, we created an orbiting cycle that turns on its own axis forever unless a phenomenon occurred and reshifts positions of the male and female savages. Our experts warned us about the possibility of this phenomenon occurring, for they say that the mind has a strong drive to correct and re-correct itself over a period of time if it can touch some substantial original historical base; and they advised us that the best way to deal with the phenomenon is to shave off the brute's mental history and create a multiplicity of phenomena of illusions, so that each illusion will twirl in its own orbit, something similar to floating balls in a vacuum. This creation of multiplicity of phenomena of illusions entails the principle of crossbreeding the nigger and the horse as we stated above, the purpose of which is to create a diversified division of labor; thereby creating different levels of labor and different values of illusion at each connecting level of labor. The results of which is the severance of the points of original beginnings for each sphere illusion. Since we feel that the subject matter may get more complicated as we proceed in laying down our economic plan concerning the purpose, reason and effect of crossbreeding horses and niggers, we shall lay down the following definition terms for future generations. Orbiting cycle means a thing turning in a given path. Axis means upon which or around which a body turns. Phenomenon means something beyond ordinary conception and inspires awe and wonder. Multiplicity means a great number. Means a globe. Crossbreeding a horse means taking a horse and breeding it with an ass and you get a dumb, backward, ass long-headed mule that is not reproductive nor productive by itself. Crossbreeding niggers mean taking so many drops of good white blood and putting them into as many nigger women as possible, varying the drops by the various tone that you want, and then letting them breed with each other until another circle of color appears as you desire. What this means is this: Put the niggers and the horse in a breeding pot, mix some asses and some good white blood and what do you get? You got a multiplicity of colors of ass backward, unusual niggers, running, tied to backward ass long-headed mules, the one productive of itself, the other sterile. (The one constant, the other dying, we keep the nigger constant for we may replace the mules for another tool) both mule and nigger tied to each other, neither knowing where the other came from and neither productive for itself, nor without each other. CONTROLLED LANGUAGE Crossbreeding completed, for further severance from their original beginning, WE MUST COMPLETELY ANNIHILATE THE MOTHER TONGUE of both the new nigger and the new mule, and institute a new language that involves the new life's work of both. You know language is a peculiar institution. It leads to the heart of a people. The more a foreigner knows about the language of another country the more he is able to move through all levels of that society. Therefore, if the foreigner is an enemy of the country, to the extent that he knows the body of the language, to that extent is the country vulnerable to attack or invasion of a foreign culture. For example, if you take a slave, if you teach him all about your language, he will know all your secrets, and he is then no more a slave, for you can't fool him any longer, and BEING A FOOL IS ONE OF THE BASIC INGREDIENTS OF ANY INCIDENTS TO THE MAINTENANCE OF THE SLAVERY SYSTEM. For example, if you told a slave that he must perform in getting out "our crops" and he knows the language well, he would know that "our crops" didn't mean "our crops" and the slavery system would break down, for he would relate on the basis of what "our crops" really meant. So you have to be careful in setting up the new language; for the slaves would soon be in your house, talking to you as "man to man" and that is death to our economic system. In addition, the definitions of words or terms are only a minute part of the process. Values are created and transported by communication through the body of the language. A total society has many interconnected value systems. All the values in the society have bridges of language to connect them for orderly working in the society. But for these language bridges, these many value systems would sharply clash and cause internal strife or civil war, the degree of the conflict being determined by the magnitude of the issues or relative opposing strength in whatever form. For example, if you put a slave in a hog pen and train him to live there and incorporate in him to value it as a way of life completely, the biggest problem you would have out of him is that he would worry you about provisions to keep the hog pen clean, or the same hog pen and make a slip and incorporate something in his language whereby he comes to value a house more than he does his hog pen, you got a problem. He will soon be in your house."

Additional Note: "Henry Berry, speaking in the Virginia House of Delegates in 1832, described the situation as it existed in many parts of the South at this time: "We have, as far as possible, closed every avenue by which light may enter their (the slaves) minds. If we could extinguish the capacity to see the light, our work would be complete; they would then be on a level with the beasts of the field and we should be safe. I am not certain that we would not do it, if we could find out the process and that on the plea of necessity."

[From Brown America, The story of a New Race by Edwin R. Embree. 1931 The Viking Press]

CHAPTER 5

How Did We Get Here?
The African, Indigenous Americans, and European Journey Through Colonization

ow did we get here? While the Transatlantic Slave Trade is often the focal point of discussions about the racial divide, the truth is that the roots of this division stretch far deeper. To fully understand how we arrived at this fractured reality, we must examine the historical, political, and spiritual forces that shaped the world we live in today—particularly in America. This chapter delves into the role of colonization, the manipulation of Christianity, and the economic and social systems that upheld slavery.

History is not just about dates and events—it is about understanding the foundations upon which societies were built. ***When we ignore history, we risk repeating its mistakes.*** Many of the issues that continue to plague America, from systemic racism to economic disparities, are directly tied to the past. The racial divide did not appear overnight; it was carefully constructed over centuries through policies, religious endorsements, and economic exploitation.

One of the earliest and most influential enablers of European colonization and slavery was the Catholic Church, which wielded immense political and religious power. While Christianity, at its core, is about love, justice, liberation and salvation, history reveals that men corrupted its teachings to serve their own desires for lustful power and wealth. The papal bulls—official decrees issued by the Pope—laid the groundwork for colonization and slavery under the guise of spreading the *so-called* Christian faith.

In 1452, Pope Nicholas V issued the Dum Diversas, which granted Portugal the right to enslave non-Christians, particularly Africans and Muslims. This decree provided moral and legal justification for the African slave trade. In 1493, Pope Alexander VI issued the Inter Caetera, which divided "newly discovered" lands between Spain and Portugal and gave them authority to conquer and convert non-Christian peoples. These papal bulls reinforced the belief that European nations had a divine right to take land, enslave people, and impose their rule on indigenous populations. This was not the gospel of Jesus Christ but a distortion of it for power and political gain.

The endorsement of slavery by religious institutions gave colonizers a moral shield. European nations—Spain, Portugal, Britain, France, and others—used Christian rhetoric to justify their brutal expansion into Africa and the Americas. This manipulation of Christianity led to the belief that Black and Indigenous people were inferior and needed to be "civilized" through forced labor, conversion, and European cultural assimilation.

The economic system of slavery was not just about free labor; it was about maintaining control. European colonizers and American slaveholders understood that to keep their system intact, they had to ensure that enslaved people remained divided. In the Willie Lynch letter, whether authentic or apocryphal (fabricated), such methods utilized by enslavers capture the essence of this divide-and-conquer strategy. It speaks of deliberately pitting enslaved people against one another, fostering mistrust and division within the Black community. The lasting effects of this psychological manipulation can still be seen today in colorism and internalized racism.

Slavery in America, unlike some forms of servitude in the ancient world, *was designed to strip people of their identity and humanity.* Families were torn apart, cultural heritage was erased, and generations were born into bondage with no hope of escape. Laws were passed to prevent enslaved people from learning to read or practicing their native religions, ensuring they remained dependent on their oppressors. Even after the abolition of slavery, systemic racism continued through sharecropping, Jim Crow laws, redlining, and mass incarceration—all designed to keep Black people economically and socially disadvantaged.

Understanding this history is not about dwelling in the past for the sake of dwelling in the past but about recognizing the foundations and the continued struggles of the present among people of color globally. The racial divide in America is not accidental; it is the result of centuries of deliberate actions, wherein the consequences are evident and felt or experienced by many, knowingly or not.

The Colonizers' Redefinition of Identity

Not only did the colonizers seek to redefine borders, but they also sought to redefine people groups and ethnicities by inserting race as a categorization tool. As previously discussed, non-Europeans were largely considered inferior, but what is particularly interesting is how European colonizers selectively applied the label of "European" or "White" based solely on physical appearance rather than ancestry or historical lineage when it was advantageous to do so. This practice was not only a means of reinforcing European dominance but also a way of controlling how people were perceived and treated within their colonial systems.

One of the most glaring examples of this racial reclassification was how European powers chose to describe several North African peoples and nations. Some lighter-skinned North Africans were categorized as "White" or "European" despite their ancestral roots being tied more closely to Africa and the Middle East than to Europe. The colonial mindset sought to create divisions by rewarding those who could pass as white with certain privileges, while darker-skinned individuals were subjected to systemic oppression. This racial reclassification has persisted into modern times, shaping identity politics, census categorizations, and even immigration policies in Western nations.

The Misclassification of North Africans and Other Non-Europeans

Historically, North Africa has been home to a diverse range of peoples, including Berbers, Arabs, Nubians, and other indigenous African groups. However, because some North Africans possessed lighter skin tones, European colonial powers often designated them as "Caucasian" or "European" in various official records. This classification was not based on ancestry but on the colonial desire to separate and elevate certain groups while subjugating others. The concept of whiteness became less about actual lineage and more about political and social benefits.

This practice was not limited to North Africa. Similar tactics were used in other regions where lighter-skinned non-Europeans were granted honorary "White" status, whether in South Africa under apartheid, in parts of Latin America, or even within the caste systems of colonial India. By doing so, European colonizers ensured that racial hierarchies remained intact, with power concentrated among those who were able to align and/or ally themselves with whiteness.

A Personal Encounter: Embracing a False Identity

I now bring to your attention a conversation with a brother in Christ and a respected acquaintance (initials P.T.), an Egyptian man whose family came from North Africa but made America their home. He was a fair-skinned individual with somewhat dark curly hair and, to some extent, European features. What struck me about our conversation on this particular occasion was how readily and confidently he defined himself as being "White." Despite his roots in Egypt, a historically African and Middle Eastern nation, he embraced a European racial identity.

This phenomenon is not unique. Many individuals from North Africa and other regions have claimed whiteness, even when historical and genealogical evidence suggests otherwise. The reasons for this are complex, but they often stem from the perceived benefits associated with whiteness—social acceptance, economic opportunities, and the ability to navigate Western institutions without the burdens of racial discrimination. European colonial powers reinforced these racial divisions by offering certain privileges to those who were able to align themselves with whiteness, even if they were not European by ancestry.

And so, it was and is; some Caucasians have also strategically labeled non-European individuals as white when it served their interests. This reclassification allowed colonial governments and white supremacist structures to maintain control by blurring racial lines in ways that benefited them. This manipulation of racial identity has had lasting effects, contributing to the complexities of race and ethnicity in modern societies.

The Lasting Impact of Racial Reclassification

The colonial redefinition of race was not merely a historical anomaly—it has ongoing consequences in global identity politics. Today, racial classifications continue to be fluid, often dictated by political, social, and economic incentives rather than historical lineage. The concept of whiteness, as shaped by European colonialism, remains a tool used to grant or deny privileges based on arbitrary physical traits.

Understanding this manipulation of identity is crucial as we continue to navigate racial dynamics in America and beyond. It sheds light on how racial divisions were engineered, maintained, and reinforced, and it challenges us to question the structures that still benefit from these artificial classifications. The erasure and redefinition of ethnic identities serve as a reminder of the psychological and spiritual warfare that continues to shape our world.

The Perversion of Biblical Truth: The Doctrine of Divine Destiny

The European colonization of Africa, the Americas, and other regions was not merely a pursuit of wealth and power—it was also justified through a distorted interpretation of Biblical truth. At the heart of this justification was the erroneous belief that Europeans had a divine mandate to rule over other peoples and lands. This ideology, supported and encouraged by church leaders, including the Catholic Church, twisted Christian doctrine to serve political and economic ambitions.

As previously stated, the origins of this perversion can be traced to the Papal Bulls of the 15th century, particularly Dum Diversas (1452) and Inter Caetera (1493). These decrees granted European monarchs—especially those of Portugal and Spain—the supposed divine right to conquer, enslave, and convert non-Christian peoples. The Papacy framed these conquests as part of a sacred mission to spread Christianity, but in reality, they facilitated immense suffering, displacement, and genocide.

The ideology of European *"Divine Destiny"* emerged from this theological distortion. Later, the ideology of *"Manifest Destiny"* also emerged from this theological perversion, where it was believed that the United States was divinely ordained to expand across the North American continent. The term "Manifest Destiny," popularized by John L. O'Sullivan in the 19th century, reflected this belief. Meanwhile, the broader concept of "Divine Destiny" has been used throughout history to justify territorial expansion and colonialism, with European powers often invoking it as a divine mandate for their imperial actions.

This ideology also influenced *"American Exceptionalism,"* the belief that the United States had a unique divine mandate to lead the world in righteousness and democracy. *[John Winthrop, a Puritan leader, 1630]*

The Myth of the "City on a Hill" and Christian Nationalism

The concept of a "City on a Hill," first articulated by Puritan leader John Winthrop in 1630, further entrenched the belief that America was divinely chosen to be a model society. Rooted in the Puritan vision of a covenant with God, this ideology suggested that America had a moral and religious obligation to spread its values across the world.

While originally intended to inspire a so-called godly society, the concept became a tool of Christian Nationalism, which fused national identity with religious supremacy. Throughout history, this belief has been used to justify colonization, racial subjugation, Manifest Destiny, and policies that prioritize a White Christian identity over others.

Christian Nationalism was and is not unique to America. European nations, including Britain, France, Spain, and Portugal, once wielded similar ideologies to justify their imperial conquests. The blending of nationalism and religious superiority led to the oppression of countless Indigenous, African, and non-European peoples.

Pseudoscience and the Justification of Racism

Beyond religious justifications, European nations had also turned to pseudoscience (*this Great Lie*) to validate racial hierarchy. Scientific racism emerged as a means to justify white supremacy, employing flawed research and biased interpretations of human biology.

- The "Great Chain of Being": A hierarchical classification that placed Europeans at the top as the most "evolved" and "civilized" race while ranking Africans and Indigenous peoples as inferior.

- Phrenology and Craniometry: These pseudosciences claimed that skull size and shape determined intelligence, reinforcing racial stereotypes.

- Social Darwinism: A misapplication of Charles Darwin's theories, Social Darwinism suggested that white Europeans were biologically destined to rule over other races.

Portugal, Spain, Britain, France, and other colonial powers used these fabricated theories to justify slavery, segregation, and colonial rule. These false sciences shaped policies, laws, and cultural attitudes, embedding racism into the very fabric of Western societies.

The Unparalleled Horror of the Transatlantic Slave Trade

While slavery or servitude had existed in various forms throughout history, the Transatlantic Slave Trade introduced an unprecedented level of brutality, dehumanization, and racial justification. Before European involvement, slavery in Africa, the Middle East, and Asia (the Afro-Asiatic region) was often based on war captivity, debt, or punishment rather than race. In many cases, enslaved individuals had rights, could integrate into society, and even achieve positions of influence.

However, the Transatlantic Slave Trade brought a uniquely *barbaric system* in which Africans were forcibly taken from their homelands, packed into ships under horrific conditions, and treated as property rather than human beings. The brutality extended beyond mere forced labor:

- The Middle Passage saw millions of Africans perish due to starvation, disease, and inhumane treatment.

- Enslaved Africans were stripped of their names, identities, and languages.

- Families were intentionally separated to break bonds of resistance.

- Extreme violence—including whippings, mutilation, and sexual exploitation—was common.

The Transatlantic Slave Trade supplied labor for America, Brazil–South America, and the Caribbean, all of which were shaped by war, conquest, and deception. Brazil, in particular, became the largest recipient of enslaved Africans, with more than 5 million Africans forcibly transported there—a number far surpassing that of North America with around 400,000. European colonizers justified their actions by portraying Africans as subhuman, using both religious distortions and pseudoscientific racism.

The Theft of Indigenous and Mexican Lands

Colonization did not stop at enslaving Africans; it also included the violent displacement of Indigenous Americans and Mexicans from their lands in Western North America. Through war, broken treaties, and forced removals, European settlers and, later, the U.S. government systematically stole vast territories from native populations.

- **The Trail of Tears (1830s):** Tens of thousands of Native Americans were forcibly relocated, resulting in mass deaths.

- **Mexican American War (1846–1848):** The U.S. seized half of Mexico's territory, including present-day California, Texas, Arizona, and New Mexico.

- **The Doctrine of Discovery:** A legal framework derived from Papal Bulls that justified European claims over non-Christian lands.

Before committing fully to the Transatlantic Slave Trade, European colonizers also attempted to enslave Indigenous Americans. While they initially exploited Native Americans for forced labor, the practice of enslaving them declined over time due to several key factors:

1. **High Mortality Rates** – Native Americans were highly susceptible to European diseases such as smallpox, measles, and influenza, which decimated indigenous populations. Unlike enslaved Africans—who had been exposed to some Old-World diseases due to earlier interactions with Europeans and Middle Easterners—Native Americans had little to no immunity. The staggering death toll made their continued enslavement less sustainable.

2. **Knowledge of the Land** – Unlike Africans, who were forcibly transported to foreign lands, Native Americans were deeply familiar with the geography. This allowed them to escape captivity more easily and seek refuge within their own tribal networks. Colonizers found it difficult to maintain control over large numbers of enslaved Indigenous people because they could often flee and rejoin their communities.

3. **Tribal Alliances and Resistance** – Many Native American groups were not isolated tribes but had extensive political and military alliances. When enslaved or threatened, some tribes retaliated with violent resistance. This made it increasingly dangerous for European settlers and later American slaveholders to rely on indigenous labor.

4. **Legal and Economic Shifts** – As European demand for enslaved labor grew, the Transatlantic Slave Trade provided an alternative source of forced labor. The African enslaved, who had already endured the horrors of being uprooted from their homelands, were seen as easier to control since they had no local support networks. Furthermore, laws were gradually put in place that formalized African slavery, making Native American enslavement less common.

5. **The Shift to Land Dispossession** – Instead of relying on Native Americans as a labor source, European colonizers and later the U.S. government found it more profitable to simply remove them from their lands. This was done through forced relocations, genocidal wars, and treaties that were repeatedly broken. Policies such as the Indian Removal Act of 1830 prioritized land seizure over indigenous enslavement, as settlers sought to expand agricultural plantations that were worked by enslaved Africans instead.

Although Native American slavery declined, it never completely disappeared. Many Native Americans were still forced into indentured servitude, subjected to debt peonage, and exploited as laborers, particularly in Spanish and later U.S. territories. However, by the late 1600s, enslaved Africans had become the dominant labor system in European colonies, with Native American lands increasingly targeted for expansion rather than their people for forced labor.

The Refuge of African Americans
Among Native Americans

As the institution of slavery entrenched itself in the American colonies (stolen lands), many African Americans, in their pursuit of freedom, sought refuge among the Native American tribes. While both enslaved African and Native Americans were systematically oppressed by European colonizers, a bond among a number of these oppressed people began to form over time that would provide some hope for freedom and survival.

Enslaved Africans who managed to escape found sanctuary in the wild and often fled to indigenous territories. Some Native American tribes, especially those in the Southeast and the Great Plains, took in runaway slaves, offering them protection from slave hunters and giving them the opportunity to forge new lives. Some enslaved Africans, upon seeking refuge with Native Americans, were not only taken in as members of the tribes, but they also intermarried (ethnic blending) with the indigenous people, becoming integrated into the tribal communities. This fostered a sense of kinship, shared struggle, and mutual resistance to the European colonizers and later American expansionist forces who held the belief in Manifest Destiny.

One such example is the formation of Maroon communities—groups of runaway slaves who escaped to form independent settlements, often living alongside Native American tribes. These communities were able to live autonomously and defend themselves against the enslavers, and some enslaved Africans even became deeply ingrained in Native American culture, language, and traditions. In some cases, these groups shared the same political and military goals, and tribes would sometimes engage in military alliances with runaway enslaved Africans to defend against colonial forces.

During the Civil War, the relationship between African Americans and Native Americans was complex. While some Native American tribes had previously aided runaway enslaved Africans, several—including the Cherokee, Creek, Seminole, and Choctaw—aligned with the Confederacy, partly due to strategic interests and historical tensions with the U.S. government. Some African Americans fought within these alliances, either as free men under pressure or as enslaved individuals. Additionally, certain Native American tribes practiced European-style slavery, holding African Americans as property.

In some cases, enslaved Africans were later granted tribal citizenship, weaving a complicated history of shared identity. However, not all tribes accepted Africans as members, and some even participated in capturing and returning runaway enslaved people to European enslavers. This intricate history reflects the diverse and sometimes contradictory interactions between Native Americans and enslaved Africans during this period.

Though the situation was fraught with complexities and challenges, it is clear that some Native Americans offered sanctuary to many enslaved Africans seeking freedom, and over time, this solidarity helped shape a shared cultural identity that transcended race. The intertwining histories of once enslaved Africans and Native Americans during colonization and slavery provide a powerful testament to resilience and survival, even amidst the darkest chapters of American history.

Yet again, by framing these acts of takeover as part of Divine destiny, European and American powers concealed their brutal conquests under the guise of righteousness. The devastation of Indigenous and Mexican communities, in part, mirrored the fate of African peoples under slavery.

A Personal Reflection on Indigenous and African American History

In concluding this chapter, I have shared a small portion of Native American or Indigenous Peoples' history, as it is an integral part of the larger American history with respect to colonization. The struggle and displacement of Native Americans—as they were pushed from their lands, faced genocide, and witnessed their cultures erased—are woven deeply into the fabric of the American experience, intertwined with the story of enslaved Africans who were brought to these shores under violent, unjust circumstances.

I felt it important to also highlight the plight, struggles, and challenges faced by Indigenous Peoples, not only because of their historical significance but also because I, an African American male, identify with them. Through DNA testing, I have traced my lineage and heritage across various regions of Africa, learning about my ancestral roots that span a vast and diverse continent. What was a surprising and humbling discovery, however, was that my DNA also traces back to Indigenous American roots.

As much as my heritage is predominantly African, there is a shared lineage with the Indigenous Peoples of this land. My ancestry includes a mixture of Native American roots, a connection I was unaware of until my DNA revelation. Moreover, European ancestry also exists within my DNA makeup, making my personal history even more complex. If only the story of my DNA could be fully explained, it would tell a story of intertwined lineages—a history marked by conquest, forced migration, cultural fusion, and survival against all odds.

This discovery has greatly enlightened me, as it bridges the histories of two oppressed peoples—those of African descent and those of Indigenous heritage—woven together in a shared experience of colonial violence, forced migration, and resilience. As I reflect on this, I realize that the struggles faced by Indigenous Americans and African Americans are not isolated stories but part of a larger narrative of colonization and racial exploitation that stretches far beyond simple borders. In many ways, the histories of both peoples are bound together by the enduring forces of oppression, and this realization has strengthened my understanding of the urgent need for solidarity and unity among all people. I will add, not a likely outcome that culminates on this side of glory amongst spiritually broken and divided people.

This chapter has sought to reflect on the past and how history still shapes the present. As I look at my own ancestry, I am reminded that no individual history is simple—it is often woven from many threads, each one carrying its own story of struggle, survival, and strength. Just as the legacy of colonization has shaped the world, it has also shaped who I am. And in telling this story, I am both a part of that greater narrative and yet an individual striving to make sense of the complexities that my heritage holds.

As we continue to move forward in this condensed historical journey of exploration and understanding, we are to be reminded that ***the past cannot and must not be forgotten, rewritten or erased***. It is through the recognition of our shared history that we can begin to heal, rebuild, and understand the deep connections that bind us as a collective, striving for justice, truth, and reconciliation.

Conclusion of Chapter 5: The Enduring Legacy of Colonization

As we draw Chapter 5 to a close, it is crucial to reflect on the far-reaching and lasting effects of colonization that continue to reverberate in our society today. Colonization, driven by the European powers and justified under the banner of twisted Christianity, not only redefined land and people groups but also created racial and ethnic divisions that have persisted for centuries. The brutal subjugation of African peoples through the incredulous Transatlantic Slave Trade, the violent displacement of Indigenous Americans, and the ideological construction of race were all components of a system designed to dehumanize and marginalize those deemed "other."

The notion of European divine destiny, which was promoted by colonial leaders and supported by the Roman Catholic Church, provided the moral justification for the conquest and exploitation of entire peoples and continents. The idea of American exceptionalism, tied to the concept of a "City on a Hill," further entrenched these ideologies, leading to the false belief that the colonizers were divinely ordained to rule over and reshape the world in their image. This doctrine not only justified slavery but also the violent removal of Indigenous peoples from their lands.

The chapter further explored how racial distinctions were used as tools of oppression. The categorization of people based on physical appearance, often in ways that defied logical or cultural boundaries, was a deliberate attempt to cement the superiority of Europeans over others. In particular, the attempt to classify North Africans and others as "White" was a distortion of both geography and ethnicity. These pseudoscientific classifications became embedded in the social fabric, influencing not just the relationships between the colonizers and the colonized, but also shaping the ways in which people of different backgrounds would be perceived and treated for generations to come.

Moreover, the story of enslaved Africans seeking refuge among Native American tribes is a testament to the solidarity between these two oppressed groups. Both enslaved African and Indigenous peoples were subjected to similar forms of violence and dehumanization, yet through their shared suffering, they also formed alliances that defied the racial and cultural divisions imposed by their oppressors. The willingness of some Native American tribes to take in runaway enslaved and grant them sanctuary highlights the potential for unity amidst division, showing that the bonds of humanity can transcend race and history when people unite for a common cause—freedom and inherent equality for all as endowed by our Creator–Yahweh.

This chapter also underscores the personal nature of history. As I reflect on my own ancestry, which includes African, Indigenous, and European roots, it serves as a powerful reminder of the complexity and interconnectedness of historical narratives. Uncovering my lineage speaks to the larger story of the African American experience as overcomers, which is shaped not only by the brutal legacy of slavery but also by the resilience of Indigenous peoples, whose cultures and histories are also often overlooked in the mainstream narrative.

Chapter 5 emphasizes that understanding the past—acknowledging the violence, the injustices, and the shared struggles—is essential for moving forward. The scars of colonization are still visible today, and healing can only begin when we confront these painful truths. By recognizing the interconnected histories of African Americans, Indigenous Americans, others and even European colonizers, we can attempt to dismantle the racial and ethnic divisions that have been constructed over time. This chapter encourages a reexamination of identity, history, and legacy, urging us to embrace a more nuanced and inclusive understanding of who we are and how we arrived at this point.

It is through this understanding that we can begin to build bridges of solidarity, honor the resilience of those who have been oppressed, and move toward a future where the cycles of oppression and injustice are broken. The story of colonization is not just a story of the past; it is a living history that continues to shape our world. And it is only by confronting that history with honesty and empathy that we can hope to create a more just and equitable society for future generations.

CHAPTER 6

Africa's Divine Connection: God's Word and Africa's Legacy

The Reliability, Origin, and Spread of the Bible

The Bible is the most well-preserved and authenticated ancient text in human history. Christians, those who are true followers of Christ, unquestionably believe that it is the divinely inspired and inerrant Word of God, revealed through prophets, apostles, and other chosen individuals, to bring forth His truth to the world. Unlike any other religious or historical book, the Bible contains fulfilled prophecies, unparalleled manuscript evidence, and archaeological support that validate its authenticity and divine origin.

The Scriptures assert their divine inspiration in passages such as 2 Timothy 3:16, which states:

"All Scripture is God-breathed and is useful for teaching, rebuking, correcting, and training in righteousness."

Similarly, 2 Peter 1:20-21 affirms:

"Above all, you must understand that no prophecy of Scripture came about by the prophet's own interpretation. For prophecy never had its origin in the human will, but prophets, though human, spoke from God as they were carried along by the Holy Spirit."

From Genesis to Revelation, the Bible presents a consistent message of God's redemptive plan for humanity, making it unique among religious texts.

The Historical Development of the Bible

The Bible was written over a span of approximately 1,500 years by more than 40 authors from diverse backgrounds, including kings, prophets, shepherds, fishermen, tax collectors, and scholars. These authors, though separated by time and geography, produced a unified message that points to God's sovereignty, righteousness, and plan for salvation.

- The Old Testament (Hebrew Bible) was written between 1400–400 BC. It consists of 39 books originally written in Hebrew and Aramaic.

- The New Testament was written between *AD 50–100* and consists of 27 books, written primarily in Greek.

The Bible's structure:

1. The Old Testament – The foundation of the Christian faith, containing the Law (Torah), historical books, poetry/wisdom literature, and prophetic writings.

2. The New Testament – The fulfillment of Old Testament prophecies, containing the Gospels, Acts, the Epistles (letters to churches and individuals), and the prophetic book of Revelation.

Manuscript Evidence: Unmatched by Any Other Ancient Text

The Bible has more manuscript evidence than any other ancient document. When compared to other historical writings, the manuscript support for the Bible is overwhelming:

- New Testament manuscripts: Over 5,800 Greek manuscripts, 10,000+ Latin manuscripts, and over 24,000 total manuscripts in various languages before the invention of the printing press.

- Old Testament manuscripts: The Dead Sea Scrolls (discovered in 1947) confirmed the accuracy of Old Testament texts, dating back as early as 250 BC.

For comparison:

- Homer's Iliad – Approximately 1,800 manuscripts, the earliest copy dating to 400 BC (500 years after its original writing).

- Julius Caesar's Gallic Wars – Only 10 manuscripts, with the earliest copy written 900 years after the original.

The Bible's unparalleled manuscript evidence ensures that what we read today is nearly identical to what was originally written.

Archaeological Evidence Supporting the Bible

Archaeology has consistently confirmed biblical narratives. Some key discoveries include:

- The Dead Sea Scrolls (1947) – Confirmed the accuracy of the Old Testament.

- The Tel Dan Inscription (1993) – The first historical evidence of King David's dynasty.

- The Pilate Stone (1961) – Confirms the existence of Pontius Pilate, the Roman governor who sentenced Jesus to crucifixion.

- The Hittite Civilization – Once thought to be a biblical myth, later confirmed by archaeological discoveries in the 19th century.

These findings demonstrate that the Bible is not a collection of myths but a historically reliable record.

The Power of Biblical Prophecy

One of the strongest proofs of the Bible's divine inspiration is fulfilled prophecy. Unlike other religious texts, the Bible contains hundreds of prophecies that have come to pass with precise accuracy.

- Messianic Prophecies: The Old Testament contains over 300 prophecies about Jesus Christ, all fulfilled in the New Testament.

- Isaiah 7:14 – The Messiah (Jesus, the Christ) would be born of a virgin.

- Micah 5:2 – The Messiah would be born in Bethlehem.

- Psalm 22 – Describes crucifixion 1,000 years before it was historically practiced.

- Israel's Restoration: Ezekiel 37 prophesied the rebirth of Israel, which occurred in 1948 after nearly 2,000 years of exile.

No other religious book contains such detailed, accurate predictions that have come to pass.

The Bible's Origin: From the Middle East to the World

The Bible's origins trace back to the Middle East, where God–Jesus Himself, revealed Himself to the Israelites. The Old Testament was written by Hebrew prophets and scribes, while the New Testament records the life, death, and resurrection of Jesus Christ and the birth of the Christian church recorded by a few of the original apostles whom Jesus specifically "Called" to follow Him.

Jesus affirmed the authority of the Old Testament and proclaimed the fulfillment of its promises through Himself. In Matthew 5:17, He states:

"Do not think that I have come to abolish the Law or the Prophets; I have not come to abolish them but to fulfill them."

Jesus and the Establishment of His Church

Jesus declared His plan to build His church in Matthew 16:18:

"And I tell you that you are Peter, and on this rock, I will build my church, and the gates of Hades will not overcome it."

We, the Church or children of God, yet continue to stand through God's Divine Providence!

After His resurrection, Jesus commissioned His followers to spread the gospel:

"Go therefore and make disciples of all nations, baptizing them in the name of the Father and of the Son and of the Holy Spirit." (Matthew 28:19)

This command led to the explosive growth of Christianity throughout the then-known world and its global continuance today.

The Spread of the Gospel and the Early Church

The book of Acts details the spread of Christianity:

- **Pentecost (Acts 2)** – The Holy Spirit empowered the apostles, leading to the conversion of 3,000 people in one day.

- **The Church in Jerusalem (Acts 2–7)** – The first Christian community formed.

- **Persecution and Expansion (Acts 8)** – Persecution scattered Believers, spreading the gospel beyond Jerusalem.

- **Antioch: The First Use of the Term "Christian" (Acts 11:26)** – In Antioch, Believers were first called "Christians," marking a distinct identity separate from Judaism.

- **Paul's Missionary Journeys (Acts 13–28)** – The gospel spread throughout the Roman Empire (the known or "civilized" world), reaching Europe, Asia Minor, and North Africa.

Through persecution and resistance, the message of Jesus Christ continued to spread, fulfilling His promise that ***His church would endure!***

The Bible's Global Influence and Its Spread to Africa

The Bible stands alone as the most complex, historically accurate, and divinely inspired book ever written. It is not the product of any single culture, race, or nation. Rather, it is the revealed Word of God, given to humanity through divinely chosen individuals from various backgrounds over multiple generations.

Unlike other religious texts that are rooted in a single cultural or ethnic origin, the Bible speaks to all people, transcending racial and geographic boundaries. Many of its writers lived in the Middle East, North Africa, and surrounding Afro-Asiatic regions—far from the Western world. This historical and geographical reality disproves the false claim that Christianity is a "white man's religion."

The Bible's Spread Throughout the Known World

The message of the Bible began with the Jewish people in the Middle East but quickly spread as purposed or prophesied beyond its initial audience.

The book of Acts records how the gospel message moved outward, reaching the far corners of the then-known world or "civilized," including Africa.

At Pentecost (Acts 2:1-12), Jews from various nations had gathered in Jerusalem, and among them were individuals from Egypt and Cyrene (modern-day Libya in North Africa):

"Phrygia and Pamphylia, Egypt and the parts of Libya near Cyrene; visitors from Rome (both Jews and converts to Judaism)." (Acts 2:10)

These individuals, having heard and received the gospel message in their own languages, carried the *Good News or gospel message of Jesus the Savior* back to their homelands, contributing to the spread of Christianity in Africa.

The Ethiopian Eunuch: The Gospel's Journey to Africa

One of the first recorded instances of the gospel being preached to an African is found in Acts 8:26-40. Philip, one of Jesus' disciples, encountered an Ethiopian eunuch, an important official in charge of the treasury of Queen Candace of Ethiopia.

This eunuch was reading the book of Isaiah but did not fully understand it. Philip explained the prophecy, revealing how it pointed to Jesus as the Messiah. The eunuch believed, was baptized, and returned to Ethiopia, likely becoming one of the first to bring Christianity to Sub-Saharan Africa.

This event suggests that the gospel reached Africa before it reached many parts of Europe. Christianity was firmly established in Egypt and North Africa long before it took root in Western nations.

Jewish Presence in Africa and Early Christianity

Historical records confirm that Jewish communities existed in Africa long before Christianity emerged. Many Jews had settled in Egypt and other parts of North Africa due to trade, exile, and diaspora movements. The presence of Jewish communities in Africa meant that when Christianity emerged as the fulfillment of Old Testament prophecies, it had a natural pathway into African societies.

Several of the early church fathers—key figures in shaping Christian theology—were from North Africa. *Tertullian* (c. 155–220 AD), *Origen* (c. 185–254 AD), and *Augustine of Hippo* (354–430 AD) were all African theologians who contributed significantly to Christian doctrine.

Simon of Cyrene: A Black Man and the Cross of Christ

A significant and often overlooked figure in the New Testament is Simon of Cyrene, a man from North Africa who was compelled to carry Jesus' cross to Golgotha (Mark 15:21, Matthew 27:32, Luke 23:26).

"They forced a man coming in from the country, who was passing by, to carry Jesus' cross. He was Simon of Cyrene, the father of Alexander and Rufus." (Mark 15:21)

Cyrene was a city in modern-day Libya, and Simon is traditionally believed to have been of African descent. Some theologians and historians see

Simon's act as symbolic of the struggles that Black people would later endure, carrying burdens imposed upon them unjustly. Whether or not this interpretation is correct, Simon's presence in the gospel narrative once again affirms the Bible's inclusivity and its connection to Africa from the very beginning.

Christianity: Not a Western Religion

The misconception that Christianity is a Western religion stems from its later adoption by European nations and its association with colonial expansion. However, as provided history shows that Christianity was deeply rooted in the Middle East and Africa long before it became dominant in Europe.

- The Bible was written in Hebrew, Aramaic, and Greek—languages of the ancient Middle Eastern and Mediterranean world.

- Christianity flourished in Egypt, Ethiopia, and North Africa centuries before it reached Northern and Western Europe.

- The first Christian kingdom in the world, under King Ezana, an African, was in Axum (modern-day Ethiopia), which officially adopted Christianity in the early 4th century—around the same time as Rome, under Emperor Constantine.

This historical reality dismantles the false notion that Christianity is the invention of European culture. Instead, the Bible itself declares that God's message is for all nations:

"After this I looked, and there before me was a great multitude that no one could count, from every nation, tribe, people and language, standing before the throne and before the Lamb." (Revelation 7:9)

The Undeniable African Presence in the Bible

The presence of Black and African individuals within the biblical narrative is undeniable. Many key figures in Scripture are either directly African, of African descent or connected to African nations. The notion that Christianity is detached from Africa is dispelled when examining biblical history and genealogy.

Prominent Africans in the Bible

1. Nimrod (Genesis 10:8-12)

- Nimrod was the grandson of Ham and the son of Cush, making him of African descent.

- He was a mighty warrior and the first recorded builder of cities, establishing the foundations of Babylon and Assyria.

2. Hagar and Ishmael (Genesis 16, 21)

- Hagar, the Egyptian servant of Sarah, bore Ishmael, the firstborn son of Abraham.

- Many scholars believe Hagar was of African descent, possibly a Black woman.

- Ishmael became the father of the Ishmaelites, who are traditionally regarded as ancestors of many Arab nations (people of color).

3. Pharaoh's Daughter (Exodus 2:5-10)

- An Egyptian princess rescued Moses from the Nile and raised him in Pharaoh's palace.

- Moses, a central figure in Israel's history, was raised within African royalty and culture.

4. Moses' Ethiopian (Cushite) Wife (Numbers 12:1)

- Moses married a Cushite woman, sometimes translated as Ethiopian.

- Miriam and Aaron spoke against this union, possibly due to cultural differences or jealousy.

5. The Queen of Sheba (1 Kings 10:1-13; 2 Chronicles 9:1-12)

- The Queen of Sheba visited King Solomon after hearing of his wisdom.

- She is traditionally linked to Ethiopia and Yemen.

- Ethiopian *tradition* holds that she bore Menelik I, believed to be the first emperor of Ethiopia and essentially the foundation figure from whom the Solomonic Dynasty traces its origins. (c. 900 BC)

6. Zerah the Ethiopian (2 Chronicles 14:9-15)

- A Cushite military leader who led a vast army against King Asa of Judah.

7. Ebed-Melech (Jeremiah 38:7-13; 39:15-18)

- A Cushite official in King Zedekiah's court who rescued Jeremiah from a cistern.

- God acknowledged his faith and promised him protection during the Babylonian conquest.

8. The Ethiopian Eunuch (Acts 8:26-40)

- A high-ranking treasurer for Queen Candace of Ethiopia.

- He encountered Philip, accepted the gospel, and was baptized, becoming one of the first recorded African converts to Christianity.

9. Simon of Cyrene and His Sons, Alexander and Rufus (Mark 15:21, Luke 23:26, Romans 16:13)

- Simon of Cyrene, a man from Cyrene (modern Libya), was compelled to carry Jesus' cross.

- The mention of his sons, Alexander and Rufus, by the Gospel writers suggests that they were known within the early church.

- Rufus is referenced in Romans 16:13, where the Apostle Paul greets him and his mother, who was esteemed in the Christian community.

- Some view Simon's act of carrying the cross as symbolic of the struggles faced by Black people throughout history, yet also as a testament to their role in God's redemptive plan.

African Lineage in the Genealogy of Jesus

The genealogy of Jesus the Christ includes individuals with African ancestry, demonstrating the diversity within His lineage.

1. Tamar (Genesis 38, Matthew 1:3)

- Tamar bore Perez and Zerah, ancestors of Jesus.
- As a Canaanite, she was a descendant of Ham, suggesting African lineage.

2. Rahab (Joshua 2, Matthew 1:5)

- A Canaanite woman who protected the Israelite spies.
- She became an ancestor of King David and part of Jesus' lineage.

3. Ruth (Book of Ruth, Matthew 1:5)

- A Moabite woman who married Boaz and became the great-grandmother of King David.
- Moabites descended from Lot, whose lineage was intertwined with ancient African nations.

4. Bathsheba (2 Samuel 11, Matthew 1:6)

- The mother of King Solomon, she was married to Uriah the Hittite.
- Hittites had connections with African and Middle Eastern peoples.

Since these women were in Jesus' lineage, and considering their diverse ancestry—including Canaanite, Moabite, and possibly Cushite blood—

this would mean that Mary, the mother of Jesus, also carried African ancestry through her genealogy.

The Ethiopian (Cushite) Connection to the House of David

The Ethiopian royal family traces its lineage back to King Solomon through Menelik I, the son of Solomon and the Queen of Sheba. This dynasty, known as the Solomonic Dynasty, ruled Ethiopia for centuries, maintaining a connection to the House of David.

The Bible and historical tradition consistently highlight the African presence, proving that Black and African people were central in God's divine plan.

The Role of Africans in the Early Church

The presence of Black and African individuals in the early church is well-documented within Scripture and Christian history. These men not only played critical roles in the spread of the gospel but also contributed significantly to Christian theology and doctrine. While the church belongs to all people, the African presence in its formation is undeniable and must be acknowledged, particularly in light of the historical distortions imposed by European colonization.

Simeon called Niger (Acts 13:1)

In Acts 13:1, Simeon, also known as Niger, is mentioned among the prophets and teachers in the church at Antioch:

"Now there were in the church that was at Antioch certain prophets and teachers; as Barnabas, and Simeon that was called Niger, and

Lucius of Cyrene, and Manaen, which had been brought up with Herod the tetrarch, and Saul." (Acts 13:1, KJV)

The name Niger is a Latin term meaning black, suggesting that Simeon was a man of African descent. Some traditions and scholars propose that he may have been from North Africa, possibly linked to the Cyrene region. There is also speculation that he could be the same Simon of Cyrene who carried Jesus' cross, though this is not definitively confirmed. Regardless, Simeon's role as a prophet and teacher in the early church underscores the active participation of Black men in the foundational Christian movement.

Lucius of Cyrene (Acts 13:1)

Lucius of Cyrene is another African leader mentioned in Acts 13:1. Cyrene was a city in modern-day Libya, North Africa, known for its Jewish population and intellectual influence. Lucius was one of the leaders in the Antioch church, a central hub for Christian missionary activity. Given that Cyrene was a prominent African city, it is reasonable to infer that Lucius was of African descent.

Early church tradition suggests that Lucius later became a bishop and missionary, playing a key role in the expansion of the gospel beyond Jewish communities. His inclusion in the list of prophets and teachers highlights the African contribution to early Christian leadership and theological development.

The Church in Alexandria, Egypt

The city of Alexandria, Egypt, was a critical center for early Christianity. It was a cosmopolitan Afro-Asian city with a significant Jewish and Greek population. Alexandria housed one of the largest libraries of the ancient world and was a hub of religious and philosophical thought.

Theological Significance:

- Alexandria was home to one of the earliest Christian schools of theology, known as the Catechetical School of Alexandria.

- The Septuagint, the Greek translation of the Hebrew Scriptures, was produced in Alexandria, making the Old Testament accessible to Greek-speaking Jews and Gentiles – Africans and other non-Jews.

- The Alexandrian Church played a pivotal role in the development of Christian doctrine, particularly in refuting heresies and shaping early Christology.

African Church Fathers and Their Contributions

Many of the early church fathers were of African descent or worked extensively in Africa. Their contributions to Christian doctrine and philosophy were foundational to theological and ecclesiastical development.

1. Tertullian (c. 155–220 AD) – Father of Latin Christianity

- Tertullian was born in Carthage (modern Tunisia, North Africa) and is often regarded as the father of Latin theology.

- He was the first Christian writer to use the term Trinity to describe the nature of God.

- His apologetic writings defended Christianity against Roman persecution and heresies.

- While the precise details of his ethnicity remain debated, his African heritage is undeniable, and some scholars suggest he may have, in fact, been a Black man.

2. Origen (c. 185–254 AD) – Theologian and Scholar

- Origen was a leading Christian scholar and theologian from Alexandria, Egypt.

- He wrote extensively on biblical interpretation, philosophy, and apologetics.

- Some traditions suggest that he may have had African ancestry, though his exact ethnicity remains uncertain.

- His contributions to the allegorical interpretation of Scripture influenced Christian thought for centuries.

3. Athanasius of Alexandria (c. 296–373 AD) – Defender of the Nicene Creed

- Athanasius, often called "The Black Dwarf" by his opponents, was a prominent bishop of Alexandria and a staunch defender of orthodox Christianity.

- He played a key role in the Council of Nicaea (325 AD), where he refuted the heresy of Arianism, which denied the divinity of Christ.

- Many historical sources indicate that Athanasius was a dark-skinned African, reinforcing the African leadership in early church doctrine.

4. Augustine of Hippo (354–430 AD) – One of the Greatest Theologians

- Born in Tagaste, Numidia (modern Algeria, North Africa), Augustine is one of the most influential Christian theologians of all time.

- His works, Confessions and The City of God, shaped Western Christian thought.

- Augustine was of Berber descent, an indigenous African people, and is considered one of the most profound African church fathers.

5. Clement of Alexandria (c. 150–215 AD)

- A theologian and scholar, Clement led the Catechetical School of Alexandria.

- His writings merged Greek philosophy and Christian doctrine, greatly influencing early Christian thought.

- Some traditions suggest that he, like Origen, may have had African heritage.

6. Cyprian of Carthage (c. 200–258 AD)

- Cyprian was bishop of Carthage, a major center of early Christianity.

- He emphasized church unity and the necessity of sacraments.

- Carthage, as part of North Africa, had strong Black and African influences, reinforcing the widespread African role in the church.

The Apostles and the Spread of Christianity in Africa

As commanded by Jesus in Matthew 28:19-20, the apostles went out into the world to preach the gospel to *all nations.* While the New Testament provides limited direct references to their missionary journeys in Africa, early church traditions and historical sources suggest that several of the apostles and early disciples took the message of Christ to the African continent.

Mark the Evangelist - Founder of Christianity in Egypt

One of the most significant figures in the establishment of Christianity in Africa is Mark the Evangelist. According to early Christian tradition, Mark, the author of the Gospel of Mark, brought Christianity to Egypt around 42 A.D., specifically to Alexandria, one of the most influential cities in the ancient world.

- Mark's Missionary Work: He is believed to have preached the gospel, performed miracles, and established the first Christian communities in Egypt.

- The Church of Alexandria: Mark's efforts led to the foundation of the Coptic Orthodox Church, which traces its origins directly to him.

- Martyrdom: Tradition holds that Mark was martyred in Alexandria by pagan authorities who opposed the spread of Christianity.

Mark's influence was monumental, as Christianity in Egypt became one of the earliest and most robust centers of Christian thought well before European influence and colonization.

Other Apostles and Disciples Who Took the Gospel to Africa

Several other apostles and early disciples are believed to have spread the gospel in different parts of Africa, according to historical traditions and early Christian writings:

1. Matthew the Apostle

- Some traditions suggest that Matthew, the author of the Gospel of Matthew, preached in Ethiopia.

- Ethiopian traditions hold that Matthew was martyred while evangelizing the region.

- His work contributed to the strong Christian presence that would later flourish in Ethiopia.

2. Simon the Zealot

- Church traditions suggest that Simon the Zealot ministered in North Africa, particularly in regions that are today Libya and Egypt.

- Some sources claim that he traveled as far as Mauritania and even possibly into Sub-Saharan Africa before being martyred.

3. Philip the Evangelist

- Philip played a critical role in the conversion of an Ethiopian official in Acts 8:26-40.

- This Ethiopian eunuch was an important official of Queen Candace of Ethiopia, and his baptism signified one of the first recorded conversions of an African to Christianity.

- Ethiopian Christian tradition suggests that this eunuch brought Christianity back to his homeland, helping to lay the foundation for the Ethiopian Christian tradition.

4. Thomas the Apostle

- While Thomas is best known for his missionary work in India, some traditions hold that he also traveled through Arabia and parts of East Africa before reaching India.

- If these traditions are accurate, Thomas would have played a role in spreading Christianity along the Red Sea trade routes that connected Africa with the Near East.

The Rise of African Christian Centers (2nd-5th Century A.D.)

As a result of early missionary efforts, Africa became one of the most significant centers of Christianity in the first few centuries of the church.

Recap:

1. Alexandria, Egypt

- As home to the Catechetical School of Alexandria, this city became a leading center of Christian scholarship and doctrine.

- The school produced major Christian theologians, Origen, Clement of Alexandria, and Athanasius.

- The Alexandrian Church played a vital role in shaping Christian doctrine, particularly in Christology and biblical interpretation.

2. Carthage, North Africa

- Carthage (modern-day Tunisia) was another early African center of Christianity.

- It became the home of influential church fathers such as Tertullian and Cyprian, who helped define Christian theology and church structure.

- The region became a major Christian stronghold before later persecution under the Roman Empire.

3. Nubia and Ethiopia

- By the 4th century A.D., Ethiopia and Nubia had established thriving Christian communities.

- The Ethiopian Orthodox Church claims direct lineage to the Ethiopian eunuch of Acts 8, and later, King Ezana of Aksum officially adopted Christianity as the kingdom's religion in the early 4th century.

- Ethiopia remained one of the longest-standing Christian nations in history, well before European colonization.

African Christianity's Influence on Global Christianity

African Christianity was not a peripheral movement; rather, it played a foundational role in shaping global Christianity.

- North African theologians like Augustine, Tertullian, and Athanasius were indeed some of the greatest minds of early Christianity.

- The African Church was a driving force in the theological debates that shaped orthodox Christian belief, including the doctrine of the Trinity and the nature of Christ.

- Monasticism, which later spread to Europe, had its roots in Egypt with the Desert Fathers, such as Anthony the Great.

African Christianity was deeply rooted long before European colonialism and was instrumental in the spread and development of Christian doctrine worldwide.

The Decline of Christianity in Africa

While Africa played a pivotal role in early Christianity, the faith experienced a decline in certain regions due to a combination of historical, political, and religious shifts. Several key factors contributed to this decline:

1. The Rise of Islam (7th Century Onward)

- One of the most significant events that led to the decline of Christianity in North Africa was the rapid expansion of Islam in the 7th century.

- Following the Arab conquests, many Christian communities were gradually absorbed or diminished due to social, political, and economic pressures.

- Though some Christian communities, such as the Coptic Church in Egypt and the Ethiopian Orthodox Church, survived, the dominance of Islam in North Africa greatly weakened Christianity's influence in the region.

2. Persecution and Marginalization

- Christian communities in Islamic-dominated regions faced discrimination, taxation (jizya), and restrictions on worship.

- Over time, many individuals and families either converted to Islam for survival or were marginalized.

- This led to a shrinking Christian population in places like Egypt, Nubia, and parts of North Africa.

3. Colonialism and Its Aftermath

- The European colonial era (19th-20th centuries) saw a resurgence of Christianity in Africa through missionary efforts. However, colonial rule often associated Christianity with foreign control, leading to resistance and the perception that Christianity was an imperialist tool.

- After independence, many African nations sought to reclaim their cultural and religious identities, causing shifts in religious affiliations.

4. The Growth of Indigenous African Religions and Syncretism

- In response to colonial Christianity, many African communities merged indigenous beliefs with Christian teachings, leading to diverse interpretations of Christianity across the continent.

- While this created vibrant, culturally rooted Christian traditions, it also led to theological challenges and departures from orthodox Christian doctrines in some cases.

The Current State of Christianity in Africa

Despite historical challenges, Christianity in Africa today is one of the fastest-growing religious movements in the world. Africa is now considered the global epicenter of Christian growth, with millions converting to Christianity every year. Several factors contribute to this resurgence:

1. Explosive Growth of Pentecostalism and Evangelical Christianity

- The charismatic and Pentecostal movements have seen rapid expansion, particularly in West Africa, East Africa, and Southern Africa.

- These movements emphasize spiritual gifts, divine healing, and personal transformation, appealing to many Africans seeking a dynamic, experiential faith.

2. African-Led Churches and Indigenous Christian Movements

- Unlike past missionary-led churches, many African nations now have powerful indigenous Christian movements that are deeply rooted in African culture and leadership.

- Churches like the Redeemed Christian Church of God (Nigeria), Zion Christian Church (Southern Africa), and the Ethiopian Orthodox Church continue to thrive.

3. Influence on Global Christianity

- African Christianity is not just growing—it is shaping the global Christian landscape.

- Many African pastors, evangelists, and missionaries are spreading the gospel worldwide, leading to the Africanization of Christianity in places like Europe and North America.

Challenges Facing Christianity in Africa Today

Despite its growth, Christianity in Africa faces significant challenges:

1. Religious Persecution and Conflict

- In nations like Nigeria, Sudan, and Somalia, Christians face persecution from extremist groups, such as Boko Haram and Al-Shabaab.

- In some regions, Christian communities struggle against oppressive laws and societal discrimination.

2. Theological Integrity and Syncretism

- The blending of indigenous African beliefs with Christianity sometimes results in theological distortions, such as the prosperity gospel or the elevation of church leaders to god-like status.

- Ensuring that Christian teachings remain biblically sound is a major challenge for African churches.

3. Economic and Political Instability

- Many African nations face poverty, corruption, and instability, which affects the church's ability to provide consistent discipleship and community support.

- The church often steps into roles of social justice, education, and healthcare, but the struggle to maintain these efforts remains an ongoing challenge.

4. Islamic Expansion and Interfaith Relations

- While Christianity is growing, Islam is also expanding, particularly in parts of West Africa and East Africa.

- Navigating Christian-Muslim relations is a critical issue, as interfaith tensions can lead to violence or societal divisions.

Conclusion of Chapter 6

The African presence in the Bible and throughout Christian history is undeniable. From the genealogical lineage of Christ to the rise of early African Christian centers, the role of Africa in the divine narrative is not an afterthought but a foundational reality. The contributions of Africans and those of African descent—Nimrod, the Cushite wife of Moses, Hagar and Ishmael, the Queen of Sheba, the Ethiopian eunuch, Simon of Cyrene, and his sons—are woven throughout the pages of Scripture. These figures serve as clear evidence that the people of Africa were intricately involved in God's plan of redemption from the very beginning.

The presence of Africans in the lineage of Christ further solidifies this truth. Through the descendants of Ham and Shem, African blood runs through the generations leading to Mary, the mother of Jesus, affirming that the Messiah was born into a lineage that included people of color. The Solomonic dynasty, believed to have extended to Ethiopia through the Queen of Sheba's union with Solomon, further connects the House of David to the African world, reinforcing Africa's role in biblical history.

In the early church, Africans played a crucial role in spreading the gospel. Simeon called Niger, Lucius of Cyrene, and the Ethiopian eunuch were among the earliest Believers and leaders in the faith. Simon of Cyrene, the man who carried the cross of Jesus, had sons who were later known in the Christian movement. Africa itself became home to one of the most significant Christian centers in Alexandria, Egypt, where some of the greatest minds of the faith emerged—Tertullian, Origen, Athanasius, and Augustine—all of whom profoundly shaped Christian theology and doctrine.

The apostles and others, following Christ's command, brought the gospel to the African continent long before Europeans ever emerged. Mark the Evangelist established the church in Egypt, laying the foundation for the Christian faith long before the European influence. Christianity flourished in Africa from the 2nd to 5th centuries A.D., leading to the rise of great Christian centers in Carthage, Nubia, and Ethiopia. African Christianity shaped global Christianity, contributing to early doctrinal formulations, theological debates, and monastic traditions.

However, the faith in Africa faced significant trials. The rise of Islam in the 7th century led to a gradual decline in many North African Christian communities, forcing Christianity to retreat into Ethiopia and other regions. The arrival of European colonialism centuries later caused further disruption, as Christianity became entangled with colonial rule, leading to resistance and the perception of the faith as a foreign imposition. Yet, despite these challenges, Christianity in Africa never truly disappeared.

Today, Christianity in Africa is experiencing unprecedented growth, particularly through the Pentecostal and evangelical movements. Indigenous African churches have risen, led by African pastors, theologians, and missionaries who continue to shape global Christianity. Yet, the faith still faces obstacles, including persecution, theological distortions, and religious tensions in regions where Christianity and Islam intersect.

Nevertheless, the resurgence of Christianity in Africa is a testament to its deep and enduring roots. ***It is not a borrowed religion—it is a faith that has been part of Africa's story since the time of the patriarchs, prophets, and apostles.*** As Africa now stands at the center of global Christianity, the challenge ahead is to ensure that its theological foundations remain strong, grounded in Biblical truth, while embracing the cultural richness of the continent.

This chapter has demonstrated that Africa's role in the Christian faith is not a side note but an integral part of God's redemptive history. The Black presence in the Bible, the African lineage of Christ, the early African church fathers, and the continued growth of Christianity in Africa all point to one truth—God's purpose for Africa and its people have always been part of His divine plan.

CHAPTER 7

Black Hebrew Israelites and Islam: Faith, Identity, and the Christian Response

Black Hebrew Israelites (BHI): A Rising Identity Among African Americans

The Black Hebrew Israelite movement consists of various groups that claim African Americans, and other people of African descent are the true descendants of the ancient Israelites. This belief largely stems from interpretations of Deuteronomy 28, which many Black Hebrew Israelites claim prophesies the Transatlantic Slave Trade as divine punishment for Israel's disobedience.

While these groups differ in doctrine, many hold the following core beliefs:

- They reject Christianity, viewing it as a manipulated faith used by European colonizers to enslave and oppress Black people.

- They believe that modern Jews are impostors and that Black people, specifically African Americans, are the true Israelites.

- Many observe strict Old Testament laws, including dietary restrictions, Sabbath observance, and Israelite feast days.

- Some accept Jesus (often referred to as Yahawashi or Yahshua), while others reject Him entirely; here we go again or redefine His identity.

Misinterpretation of Scripture by Black Hebrew Israelites

Black Hebrew Israelites frequently cite the following scriptures to support their claims. However, proper Biblical exegesis reveals how these texts have been taken out of context or misapplied:

1. Deuteronomy 28:68 – **"And the Lord shall bring thee into Egypt again with ships, by the way whereof I spake unto thee, Thou shalt see it no more again: and there ye shall be sold unto your enemies for bondmen and bondwomen, and no man shall buy you."**

- Claim: Black Hebrew Israelites argue that this verse predicts the Transatlantic Slave Trade, with "Egypt" symbolizing bondage.

- Counter: In context, this prophecy refers to Israel's disobedience leading to captivity—historically fulfilled when Israelites were taken as prisoners by Assyrians and Babylonians. The Bible does not equate "Egypt" with America's slavery and elsewhere or suggest that Black people exclusively fulfill this prophecy.

2. Amos 9:7 – **"Are ye not as children of the Ethiopians unto me, O children of Israel? Saith the Lord. Have not I brought up Israel out of the land of Egypt? and the Philistines from Caphtor and the Syrians from Kir?"**

- Claim: Some Black Hebrew Israelites interpret this as proof that Israelites were a Black-skinned people.

- Counter: The context of the passage is metaphorical, drawing a comparison between Israel and other nations rather than making a racial statement.

3. Revelation 1:14-15 – **"His head and his hairs were white like wool, as white as snow; and his eyes were as a flame of fire; And his feet like unto fine brass, as if they burned in a furnace; and his voice as the sound of many waters."**

- Claim: This description of Jesus is used to argue that He was Black, emphasizing "woolly" hair and "burnt brass" skin.

- Counter: The passage is symbolic, describing Christ's divine glory rather than His physical appearance. The whiteness of His hair symbolizes wisdom (Daniel 7:9), and the brass-like feet reflect His refined and tested nature.

Key Scriptures Black Hebrew Israelites Misinterpret

1. Matthew 15:24 – **"But he answered and said, I am not sent but unto the lost sheep of the house of Israel."**

- Misinterpretation: Black Hebrew Israelites use this verse to argue that Jesus' message of salvation was only for Israel, which they claim refers exclusively to Black people.

- Proper Context: Jesus initially ministered to Israel, fulfilling God's promise to the Jews. However, His mission extended to the Gentiles – Africans and all others (see Matthew 28:19, Acts 10:34-35). Matthew 15:21-28 records Jesus healing the Canaanite woman's daughter because of her faith, demonstrating that salvation is not limited to Israel alone.

2. Matthew 5:17 – **"Think not that I am come to destroy the law, or the prophets: I am not come to destroy, but to fulfill."**

- Misinterpretation: Black Hebrew Israelites claim this proves that the Mosaic Law (ceremonial and kosher–dietary) laws are still in effect and must be followed.

- Proper Context: Jesus fulfilled the Law (ceremonial or sacrificial law) by being the perfect sacrifice for sin (Hebrews 10:1-10). The ceremonial and sacrificial aspects of the Law are no longer required (Colossians 2:14-17). While God's moral standards remain, salvation comes through faith in Christ, not the works of the Law (Galatians 3:24-25).

3. Romans 10:12-13 – **"For there is no difference between the Jew and the Greek: for the same Lord over all is rich unto all that call upon him. For whosoever shall call upon the name of the Lord shall be saved."**

- Misinterpretation: Black Hebrew Israelites reject this verse, claiming "Greek" only refers to Hellenized "African or Black Jews" rather than non-Israelites or gentile people.

- Proper Context: Paul explicitly states that there is no distinction between Jews and Gentiles when it comes to salvation. This contradicts the Black Hebrew Israelite doctrine that only Israel (Black people) can be saved. The term "Greek" refers to actual non-Jews, reinforcing the universal offer of salvation in Christ.

Different Sects of Black Hebrew Israelites

Within the Black Hebrew Israelite movement, several factions have emerged, each with distinct doctrines and practices.

1. Mainline Black Hebrew Israelites – These groups focus on cultural identity and emphasize Torah observance without openly hostile rhetoric.

2. Radical and Extremist Black Hebrew Israelite Groups – These factions are known for racial exclusivity and aggressive street preaching.

- Israel United in Christ (IUIC) – A well-organized group emphasizing strict legalism and Black Hebrew identity.

- Sakari – A militant group known for confrontational public debates.

- Great Millstone (GMS) – An extremist sect that promotes harsh racial ideologies.

3. African Hebrew Israelites of Jerusalem – This community was founded in the 1960s by Ben Ammi Ben Israel, who led a group of African Americans from the U.S. to Dimona, Israel.

- Today, around 3,000 members reside in Dimona and other Israeli towns.

- Though initially viewed as illegal immigrants, they have since gained permanent residency but are still not recognized as Jewish by mainstream Judaism.

- They maintain a communal lifestyle, adhering to dietary laws, Hebrew customs, and a belief in their ancestral connection to biblical Israel.

Black Hebrew Israelites vs. Mainstream Judaism

Black Hebrew Israelites and Judaism differ significantly:

- Ancestry – Judaism follows a maternal lineage or conversion process as outlined in the Old Testament, originating with the twelve tribes of Israel, while Black Hebrew Israelites claim an inherent identity as the true Jews.

- Religious Texts – Judaism follows the Torah (the first five books of the Bible) and Talmud, while Black Hebrew Israelites reject the Talmud (nonconical Rabbinic teachings).

- Jesus & The New Testament – Most Jews reject Jesus, while some Black Hebrew Israelites acknowledge Him as a Black Messiah.

Christianity vs. Black Hebrew Israelite Beliefs

The differences between Christianity and Black Hebrew Israelite teachings are vast:

- Salvation – Christianity teaches salvation through faith in Jesus Christ for all people (Romans 10:12-13). Many Black Hebrew Israelites believe salvation is only for Israel (Black people) (Matthew 15:24, misinterpreted).

- The Law – Christians believe Jesus fulfilled the Law (Matthew 5:17), whereas Black Hebrew Israelites claim the Law remains binding.

- Gentiles – Christianity embraces all nations in God's redemptive plan, while radical Black Hebrew Israelites exclude other races.

The Impact of European Colonization on African American Religious Identity

As a result of European colonization and the distortion of biblical truths, colonizers perverted Scripture to justify slavery and oppression. This corruption of Christianity led many African Americans—both those who were once Christians and others seeking so-called spiritual truth—to reject Christianity, viewing it as a distorted white man's religion. The Bible is clear, "God's "chosen people" are the Jews who are descendants of Jacob's son – hence the twelve tribes of Israel. Nevertheless, it's not beyond reason that *some* Black's ancestry may very well be traced back to Jacob's sons.

Islam and the African American Experience

Just as the Black Hebrew Israelite movement has attracted African Americans seeking an identity apart from Christianity, Islam—particularly in the form of Sunni Islam and the Nation of Islam (NOI)—has also gained a following among African Americans. This shift also often stems from a rejection of Christianity as a "white man's religion," a perception reinforced by the historical role of European colonizers and enslavers who misused Scripture to justify oppression.

Islam has particularly appealed to those seeking a sense of discipline, unity, and cultural heritage that was stripped away during slavery. However, despite its growing popularity, Islam—especially its Qur'anic reinterpretations of biblical narratives—presents serious contradictions when compared to the Bible.

Who Was Muhammad?

Muhammad ibn Abdullah's birth in 570 AD (death 632 AD), centuries after *Christianity was birth/established,* the New Testament was written, and approximately **200 years prior, the Judeo-Christian Bible was canonized** before he was born in Mecca, Arabia. And who is regarded by Muslims as the final prophet of God, receiving the Qur'an through divine revelation. However, his early life and supposed prophetic calling raise critical issues when analyzed against biblical truth:

- Upbringing: Muhammad was orphaned at a young age and raised by his uncle in a polytheistic Arab society that worshiped over 300 deities at the Kaaba in Mecca.

- Alleged Revelation: Around the age of 40, Muhammad claimed to have received visions from the angel Jibril (Gabriel), instructing him to proclaim *a new* monotheistic faith.

- Contradictions with Scripture: The Bible warns that anyone who brings a new gospel is accursed:

- Galatians 1:8 – **"But though we, or an angel from heaven, preach any other gospel unto you than that which we have preached unto you, let him be accursed."**

- This directly refutes Muhammad's claim of receiving a new divine message.

- Allegations of Demonic Influence: Muhammad himself feared he was possessed after his first visions and attempted suicide multiple times (as recorded in early Islamic texts such as Ibn Ishaq's "Sirat Rasul Allah").

Muhammad's teachings ultimately led to the establishment of Islam, which spread rapidly throughout the Middle East, North Africa, and later, parts of Europe and Asia. However, his message conflicts significantly with the teachings of Jesus the Christ and the Gospel of salvation.

Borrowed and Distorted Biblical Narratives in the Qur'an

The Qur'an, written centuries after the Bible, borrows heavily from biblical figures and stories but distorts key theological points. Here are a few major contradictions:

1. The Nature of God

- Islam: Tawhid (absolute monotheism) – Denies the Trinity and divinity of Christ.

Bible:

- John 1:1, 14 – **"In the beginning was the Word, and the Word was with God, and the Word was God... And the Word was made flesh, and dwelt among us."**

- Matthew 28:19 – Jesus commands baptism **"in the name of the Father, Son, and Holy Spirit,"** affirming the triune nature of God. (Also see: Genesis 1:1,2 & 26; John 14:16,17; Mathew 3:16,17; 2 Corinthians 13:14)

2. Jesus Christ in Islam vs. the Bible

Islam:

- Jesus (Isa) is a prophet but not divine.

- He was not crucified—instead, someone else was made to look like Him (Surah 4:157).

- He will return, not as the Lord and Savior, but to declare Islam as the true religion.

Bible:

- John 14:6 – **"I am the way, the truth, and the life: no man cometh unto the Father, but by me."**

- 1 Corinthians 15:3-4 – **"Christ died for our sins according to the scriptures; And that he was buried, and that he rose again the third day according to the scriptures."**

The Qur'an's rejection of Christ's death and resurrection directly contradicts *the core of the Gospel – the Redemption message,* proving that Islam is not a continuation of Biblical truth but a distortion of it.

3. The Role of Muhammad vs. Jesus

- Islam: Muhammad is the last prophet (Surah 33:40).

- Bible: Jesus is the **Great Prophet** and the **final revelation** of God to mankind:

- Hebrews 1:1-2 – **"God, who at sundry times and in divers manners spake in time past unto the fathers by the prophets, Hath in these last days spoken unto us by his Son…"**

Thus, no prophet—Muhammad or otherwise—can come after Christ with a "new" revelation.

Islam's Appeal to African Americans

Just as many African Americans left or have rejected Christianity for Black Hebrew Israelite ideology, others embraced Islam as an alternative, believing it to be a more authentic, non-European faith. Several factors contributed to this shift:

1. **Perceived Connection to African Heritage** – Islam was widespread in West Africa before the Transatlantic Slave Trade, leading some to reclaim it as their ancestral faith.

2. **Rejection of Christianity** – Many saw Christianity as the religion of oppressors, misused by European colonizers and slave masters.

3. **The Influence of the Nation of Islam (NOI)** – Leaders like Elijah Muhammad and Malcolm X promoted Islam as a source of empowerment for Black Americans, though NOI's doctrines are distinct from orthodox Sunni Islam.

However, despite its appeal, Islam is not biblically consistent, nor does it provide *true salvation—which is only found in Jesus the Christ.*

Christianity vs. Islam: Key Differences

Doctrine	Christianity (Biblical Truth)	Islam (Qur'anic Belief)
God's Nature	One God in Three Persons (Father, Son, Holy Spirit)	Strict monotheism, no Trinity
Jesus Christ	Son of God, divine, crucified, resurrected	A prophet, not divine, not crucified
Salvation	By grace through faith in Jesus Christ (Ephesians 2:8-9)	By works and obedience to Islamic law
Atonement for Sin	Jesus' death and resurrection (Romans 5:8)	No atonement—each must earn salvation
Scriptures	Bible (God's inspired, final Word)	Qur'an claims to correct the Bible

The Qur'an and Islam stand in ***direct opposition*** to the Old Testament, which points to the New Testament and the Gospel of Jesus the Christ, making it impossible for Islam to be a continuation of biblical revelation.

The Historical Role of Colonization and Christianity

Just as Black Hebrew Israelites emerged in response to European misuse of Scripture, many African Americans turned to Islam for similar reasons. However, it's critical to recognize:

- Christianity itself was not the oppressor—it was the perversion of Christianity by lustful and prideful colonizers that distorted Biblical truths.

- The true message of Jesus Christ is one of salvation, not oppression.

- Rejecting true Christianity based on the actions of false Christians only leads to embracing false belief systems.

Jesus Christ is the ultimate revelation of God, meaning no prophet, including Muhammad, can bring a new message that supersedes the Gospel. Furthermore, Christianity teaches that the God of the Judeo-Christian Bible is a loving, personal God who desires a relationship with humanity– the people of His making. Through the Holy Spirit, God dwells with Believers, guiding, comforting, and empowering them in their faith.

John 14:16-17 states, **"And I will pray the Father, and he shall give you another Comforter, that he may abide with you forever; Even the Spirit of truth; whom the world cannot receive, because it seeth him not, neither knoweth him: but ye know him; for he dwelleth with you, and shall be in you."**

Islam, however, does not view Allah, their god, as the personal and loving God of the Bible, who indwells His people, *because those of this world are unable to receive God - Yahweh's Truth that is spiritual in nature, even as God Himself is the Sovereign Spirit Being and Creator of all*.

Instead, Allah of the Muslim religious faith remains distant and unknowable, which stands in stark contrast to the intimate relationship the biblical and loving God offers through Jesus, additionally *through His indwelling Spirit within the souls of the true children of God the Father.*

The contrast between early Christianity and the Muslim faith (which was also embraced by Africans before their enslavement in America) is quite distinct. But here's another significant difference between the two beliefs: Christianity is a message of love–for **"God is Love"** (1 John. 4:7,8 &16; Romans 5:8). After Pentecost (Acts Chapter 2), the *Good News of Jesus* was spread throughout the world because of the Christian's love for Jesus and their fellowman, and not by might. In contrast, the spread of Islam was primarily the result of intimidation and bloody military campaigns.

Closing for Chapter 7

Throughout this chapter, we have examined the two dominant religious movements—Black Hebrew Israelite beliefs and Islam—that many African Americans have embraced in place of Christianity. Both movements emerged as a response to the historical perversion of Scripture by European colonizers and enslavers, who distorted biblical truth to justify oppression and their lustful pride. This misuse of Christianity led many to question its legitimacy, prompting them to seek alternative spiritual identities. However, despite their claims to be rooted in biblical faith, both Black Hebrew Israelite doctrines and Islam diverge significantly from the teachings of the Judeo-Christian Scriptures.

The Black Hebrew Israelite movement is not a monolithic group but consists of various sects, ranging from those who peacefully emphasize Black identity in the biblical narrative to more radical factions that espouse racial superiority and distorted interpretations of Scripture. While their claim to be the true descendants of Israel is central to their identity, their selective reading of the Bible and rejection of core Christian doctrines— such as salvation through Christ alone—places them outside of biblical orthodoxy. Many Black Hebrew Israelites misinterpret passages such as

Matthew 15:24, Romans 10:12-13, and Matthew 5:17, using them to support exclusivist views that contradict the all-encompassing message of salvation offered in Christ. Their rejection of the deity of Jesus Christ and the New Covenant undermines the very foundation of biblical faith.

Similarly, Islam presents itself as a faith of empowerment and restoration for many African Americans disillusioned with Christianity. However, its theological framework is fundamentally opposed to biblical truth. Muhammad, the founder of Islam, claimed to receive divine revelation, yet his teachings contradict the core message of the Gospel. The Qur'an borrows from the Bible but distorts key doctrines, denying the divinity of Christ, His crucifixion, and His role as the final revelation of God. Furthermore, Islam's strict monotheism rejects the personal nature of God as revealed in Christianity. Unlike the distant and unknowable Allah of Islam, the God of the Bible is a loving, personal Father who indwells His people through the Holy Spirit, offering a relationship that Islam does not provide.

Both Black Hebrew Israelite beliefs and Islam have gained traction among African Americans seeking identity, dignity, and purpose, particularly in response to the historical misrepresentation of Christianity. However, while the abuses of so-called Christian colonizers and enslavers are undeniable, their distortions of Scripture do not change the truth of God's Word. Christianity is not a religion of oppression but of liberation through Jesus Christ. The same Bible that was twisted by enslavers to justify bondage was also the source of freedom and deliverance for those who truly understood its message, *The Good News* that yet remains the same today, the message of *Salvation*. In America specifically, the rejection of Christianity in favor of these alternative movements is, at its core, a reaction to historical injustice rather than an examination of biblical truth itself.

Ultimately, African Americans—and all people—must return to the true Gospel, which transcends race, ethnicity, and historical misuse. Christianity is not a European construct; it is the faith that began in the Middle East, spread throughout Africa and the Afro-Asiatic region long before European colonization, and remains the only path to reconciliation with God. Neither Black Hebrew Israelite doctrine nor Islam offers the redemptive power of Jesus Christ. The truth remains that salvation is found in Christ alone, and it is through Him that all people—regardless of ethnicity—can find their true identity and eternal hope.

CHAPTER 8

Restoring the Image: The Need for Redemption and Justice for All

It is of utmost importance that we recognize that every person, regardless of ethnicity, tribe, nation, or whatever the association, is created in the image of God. As His Imago Dei, we are His representatives, bearing His likeness and designed to reflect His glory. However, because of our inherent sin nature, all of humanity has fallen short of the grace of God and is in desperate need of salvation through Jesus Christ. Romans 3:23 affirms this truth: **"For all have sinned, and come short of the glory of God."** This includes every ethnicity, every nation, and every people throughout history.

Although this book has underscored the evil of white colonizers and their cruel mistreatment of people of color—many of whom, now their offspring, today's whites in the year 2025 continue to wrongfully and even sinfully view themselves as a superior race. However, we must also acknowledge that sin is not exclusive to any one group of people. Ecclesiastes 7:20 states, **"For there is not a just man upon earth, that doeth good, and sinneth not."**

Throughout history, all people, cultures, and nations have committed evil, with some being more egregious than others in the sight of God. Yet, despite humanity's failings, *God's redemptive plan is available to all.* Romans 10:12-13 declares, **"For there is no difference between the Jew and the Greek: for the same Lord over all is rich unto all that call upon him. For whosoever shall call upon the name of the Lord shall be saved."**

The Christian Call to Righteousness

While the fight for justice and inherent human rights is noble, as followers of Christ, we are held to a higher standard while seeking out the righteousness and justice of God. Our rights in God do not give us a license to sin or to repay evil with evil. Jesus Himself commands in Matthew 5:44, **"But I say unto you, Love your enemies, bless them that curse you, do good to them that hate you, and pray for them which despitefully use you, and persecute you."** The world may justify retaliation, but God calls His people to a different path—one of righteousness, mercy, and grace.

This does not mean we ignore injustice, but rather, we pursue justice through the wisdom and righteousness of God, not through the sinful ways of man. Micah 6:8 states, **"He hath showed thee, O man, what is good; and what doth the Lord require of thee, but to do justly, and to love mercy, and to walk humbly with thy God?"** Our ultimate goal is not merely the restoration of earthly rights but the eternal salvation of souls.

The Universal Need for Salvation

We are all God's imagers—the saved and unsaved alike. But for those who are unsaved, their need for reconciliation with God has yet to be realized.

Just as the redeemed have received atonement through the blood of Jesus, so too does the unbeliever need this same grace to be included in God's kingdom. Jesus declared in John 14:6, **"I am the way, the truth, and the life: no man cometh unto the Father, but by me."** There is no other path to salvation, no other means of restoration apart from Christ.

Regardless of race, nationality, or historical grievances, every person stands in need of redemption. 2 Peter 3:9 confirms that God's desire is for all to come to repentance: **"The Lord is not slack concerning his promise, as some men count slackness; but is longsuffering to us-ward, not willing that any should perish, but that all should come to repentance."** The Gospel is universal, extending to all who will receive it. Salvation is not bound by ethnicity or lineage but by faith in Jesus the Christ alone.

Created to Represent God: Ambassadors on Earth

As imagers of God, we are created to represent Him as His ambassadors on earth. This role is not just a calling but a divine purpose—to reflect His glory, character, and truth in a world marred by sin. Every action, every word, every thought should echo the righteousness of God. While we live as His representatives in this temporary world, we also await our eternal destination with Jesus the Christ, our Savior, in the new heaven and new earth. 2 Corinthians 5:20 affirms our role as His ambassadors: **"Now then we are ambassadors for Christ, as though God did beseech you by us: we pray you in Christ's stead, be ye reconciled to God."** Our purpose as Believers is clear—to show the world what it means to be reconciled to God and to extend that reconciliation to others, regardless of their ethnicity, background, or status.

The Cry for Justice: Black Lives Matter

In our current context, as provided within this book, the cry of Black Lives Matter has gone out. It is crucial to understand that this cry is not rooted in any particular political agenda but rather in the fundamental plea for recognition, dignity and equality. This cry expresses that Black lives are of value, that we are not an inferior race, and that we, as people created in God's image, are inherently equal to all others in the sight of God. While the slogan has been co-opted by various movements, the core sentiment remains: *We matter!* The Bible teaches us that all humanity is created in God's image and that every person, regardless of race, is valuable in His sight. Genesis 1:27 tells us, **"So God created man in his own image, in the image of God created he him; male and female created he them."** This foundational truth underscores the inherent worth of every person, particularly in the context of the fight for justice.

However, this cry for recognition does not give anyone a right to pursue justice through unrighteous means. As we seek justice, we must ensure that our actions align with the righteousness of God. It is through His will that true justice is sought, not through sin or lawlessness. As God's ambassadors, we must represent His character in every aspect of our lives, including the fight for justice and equality.

The Challenge of Christian Liberty and the Danger of Lawlessness

While the pursuit of justice and inherent rights is noble, there are troubling signs within the Christian community that need to be addressed. Some Christians, perhaps misunderstanding their liberty in Christ, have taken Christian freedom too far. In doing so, they believe that their Christian liberty grants them the right to do whatever pleases them, even if it contradicts the truth of God's Word. The Bible is clear: Christian liberty is not a license to sin or to engage in lawlessness. 1 Peter 2:16 reminds us, **"As free, and not using your liberty for a cloak of maliciousness, but as the servants of God."** Christian liberty should not be used as an excuse to live in disobedience to God's commands.

The Gospel message is one of repentance from sin. It calls all people, regardless of race or background, to turn from their lawlessness and receive the grace and redemption offered through the blood of Jesus the Christ. Matthew 4:17 records Jesus' call to repentance: **"From that time Jesus began to preach, and to say, Repent: for the kingdom of heaven is at hand."** This message of repentance is central to the Christian faith—*it is the foundation upon which the Kingdom of God stands* – a kingdom without borders or discrimination based on skin color. Without heartfelt sorrow and repentance, there can be no reconciliation with God.

Unity Under Christ: The Gospel Message for All People

As we seek our inherent rights under God our Creator, it is vital to remember that the Gospel of Jesus the Christ transcends earthly divisions of whatever sort. While the pursuit of justice is important*, it is through Christ that true unity is found.* The message of the Gospel is one of reconciliation, both with God and with one another. Ephesians 2:14-16 teaches us that Christ has broken down the dividing walls of hostility and has created unity through His sacrifice: **"For he is our peace, who hath made both one, and hath broken down the middle wall of partition between us; having abolished in his flesh the enmity, even the law of** commandments contained in ordinances; for to make in himself of twain one new man, so making peace."

This reconciliation is not just spiritual but social. Through Christ, all Believers, regardless of their ethnicity or background, are united as *one body in Christ.* Galatians 3:28 affirms that in Christ, there is no division based on race, gender, or social standing: **"There is neither Jew nor Greek, there is neither bond nor free, there is neither male nor female: for ye are all one in Christ Jesus."** This unity is essential as we pursue justice and equality, ensuring that we do so in alignment with God's will and with love for all people.

The Gospel's Call: Atonement, Repentance, and Restoration

At the heart of the Gospel message is the atonement of Jesus Christ, which brings reconciliation and restoration to all who believe. Christ died for our sins, for our lawlessness, so that we may be brought back into the family or kingdom of God. Romans 5:8 reminds us of God's love through Christ's sacrifice: **"But God commendeth his love toward us, in that, while we were yet sinners, Christ died for us."** The atonement is a free gift, not based on our works, but based on God's grace. *Yet, this grace calls us to live in obedience, to reflect His righteousness, and to work toward His Kingdom's values.*

As we seek justice and stand for the inherent rights of all people, we must do so in a way that honors God. We must resist the temptation to live in lawlessness, for our liberty in Christ is not a license to sin. Instead, we must embrace the Gospel's call to repentance and unity under Christ, knowing that in Him, we find both justice and reconciliation. Our fight for righteousness must always be pursued with humility, love, and a commitment to God's truth so that His name may be glorified in all that we do.

Final Thought: Justice, God's Kingdom, and Our Eternal Hope

Justice may evade us in this world. Many have, many are, and many will continue to experience the injustices and evil of this fallen and broken world caused by mankind's sinful nature and the influence of malevolent evil and wicked principalities, as Scripture has clearly informed us. We are not exempt from this reality. Ephesians 6:12 reminds us: **"For we wrestle not against flesh and blood, but against principalities, against powers, against the rulers of the darkness of this world, against spiritual wickedness in high places."**

This verse reinforces that much of the suffering and injustice we experience is tied to spiritual forces operating in the unseen realm that seek to derail God's plan for humanity. These dark powers seek to influence all whom they can. Despite this, we as children of God must hold firm to our faith that God is Sovereign and indeed a just God and that He will ultimately reward or punish those who do evil. He will also reward those who do good, living out their faith to the praise and glory of God.

The call to stand firm in God's justice is echoed in Romans 2:6, which says: **"Who will render to every man according to his deeds."** This reminder affirms that, though justice may feel delayed in this life, God will bring about a perfect judgment, one that aligns with His righteousness. In the midst of injustice, we can trust that God sees all and He will make all things right in His time.

Acts 17:26 and God's Sovereignty Over All Nations

In Acts 17:26, we read: **"And (*God*) hath made of one blood all nations of men for to dwell on all the face of the earth, and hath determined the times before appointed, and the bounds of their habitation."** This passage reinforces the truth that all people, regardless of "race," ethnicity, or nationality, have one common Creator—God. He has sovereignly determined our times and boundaries, and while we may be divided by these human distinctions in the world, in God's kingdom, these disruptive divisions are erased. God's justice extends to all peoples, and His desire is that all people come to the knowledge of Him, regardless of their earthly distinctions.

Complementary scripture reinforces the same truth. Revelation 7:9 says: **"After this I beheld, and, lo, a great multitude, which no man could number, of all nations, and kindreds, and people, and tongues, stood before the throne, and before the Lamb, clothed with white robes, and palms in their hands."** This passage clearly indicates that God's kingdom is for all people, no matter their background. In Christ, people from every nation, tribe, and language will be united in worshiping Him in His eternal kingdom. This vision of unity under Christ should give us hope and remind us that our true identity is not defined by earthly distinctions but by our relationship with Jesus Christ.

Our True Identity in Christ

Who we are or who we think we are does not define us in God's eyes. These temporal and temporary identifiers will not matter in the eternal kingdom of God. Philippians 3:20 reminds us of our true citizenship: **"For our conversation is in heaven; from whence also we look for the Saviour, the Lord Jesus Christ."** As Believers in Jesus, our ultimate citizenship is in heaven, and we are sojourners here on earth, passing through a troubled and troubling world that is not our home. The Apostle Peter further affirms this in 1 Peter 2:11: **"Dearly beloved, I beseech you as strangers and pilgrims abstain from fleshly lusts, which war against the soul."** Our true home is in the presence of God, where there will be no injustice, no evil, no suffering, a world without end!

God's Kingdom: A Kingdom for All People

In God's eternal kingdom, the distinctions that divide us here on earth will be no more. We are united in Christ, and His kingdom is for people of all nations. Revelation 21:4 paints a beautiful picture of the eternal state: **"And God shall wipe away all tears from their eyes; and there shall be no more death, neither sorrow, nor crying, neither shall there be any more pain: for the former things are passed away."** In God's kingdom, there will be perfect justice, righteousness, and peace. In this kingdom, all people—those of every tribe, nation, and language—will dwell in harmony, free from the corruption and pain that afflict this fallen world.

As we, the children of God, pass through this world as sojourners, we are united with Jesus the Christ. Ephesians 2:19-20 reminds us: **"Now, therefore, ye are no more strangers and foreigners, but fellow citizens with the saints, and of the household of God; And are built upon the foundation of the apostles and prophets, Jesus Christ himself being the chief cornerstone."** For the redeemed, our identity is now rooted in Christ, and our hope is in His eternal kingdom, where justice and peace reign forever.

Though justice may evade us in this world, we hold fast to the promise that, in the eternal kingdom of God, righteousness will reign. There, all things will be made right, and every tear will be wiped away. Until that day, we continue to live as ambassadors of Christ, looking forward to the day when His justice, peace, and righteousness will fill the new earth as the waters cover the sea.

Closing Remarks

The journey of African Americans in the United States has been marked by immense struggle, resilience, and, for many, a quest for identity. From the brutal realities of slavery to the systemic injustices that persist today, the pain and suffering endured by people of color have left deep wounds, not only in our communities but in the very fabric of this nation. In the search for spiritual truth, many have rejected or turned away from Christianity, believing it to be the white man's religion—a tool of oppression rather than liberation. This rejection has led some to embrace the Black Hebrew Israelite movement, seeking identity and historical validation through an alternate lens. Others have found solace in Islam, drawn by its message of justice and resistance against oppression. While these paths are often taken in response to the misuse of Christianity by colonizers and enslavers, the tragic irony is that these very distortions have obscured the true Biblical message—a message of freedom, unity, and redemption for all people.

Yet, even in the face of these struggles, there are those among White communities who acknowledge the historical injustices inflicted upon African Americans and who empathize with our plight. They recognize that the misuse of Christianity does not define its truth. The gospel of Jesus Christ is not the possession of any one race or ethnic group; it is the message of God's love and redemption for all humanity. When we strip away the lies, the distortions, and the historical perversions of Biblical truth, we find that we are all one people—created in the image of God, loved equally by our Creator. Our differences in skin color, culture, and background do not divide us in the eyes of the Almighty; rather, they testify to the beauty of His creation.

Let us not be deceived by the heresies and lies of men, nor be bound by the chains of history that have sought to divide us. Instead, let us reclaim Biblical truth, standing firm in the knowledge that God's love transcends race, ethnicity, and human constructs. Countless, both the living and those who have fallen asleep in the Lord Jesus are and so can you be, His imagers, His people, and His redeemed if only you embrace Jesus as your Lord and Savior, the **One** who gave Himself as a sacrifice for your sins and mine.

Benediction

May the God of all nations, who formed us in His image and called us to be His own, heal the wounds of division and restore His truth in our hearts. May we walk in the light of Christ, rejecting the falsehoods that have sown discord, and embrace the unity that comes through Him alone. May His grace abound in us, His love guide us, and His peace sustain us, as we live out the calling to be one body, one family, and one people within His eternal kingdom.

In the name of Jesus Christ, the Risen King, Amen.